Novel
Interiors

Novel Interiors

Living in Enchanted Rooms Inspired by Literature

LISA BORGNES GIRAMONTI

Photographs by Ivan Terestchenko
Foreword by David Netto

POTTER STYLE
NEW YORK

Copyright © 2014 by Lisa Borgnes Giramonti
Photographs © 2014 by Ivan Terestchenko

Published in the United States by Potter Style, an imprint of the Crown Publishing Group,
a division of Random House LLC, a Penguin Random House Company, New York.
www.potterstyle.com
www.crownpublishing.com

POTTER STYLE and colophon are registered trademarks of Random House LLC.

Library of Congress Cataloging-in-Publication Data
Giramonti, Lisa Borgnes.
Novel interiors / Lisa Borgnes Giramonti. — First Edition.
pages cm
Includes index.
1. Interior decoration—Themes, motives. 2. Interior decoration in literature. I. Title.
NK2113.G57 2014
747—dc23
2013036923

ISBN: 978-0-385-34599-6
eBook ISBN: 978-0-385-34600-9

Printed in China

Design by Ashley Tucker
Cover design by Jim Massey and Ashley Tucker
Cover photographs by Ivan Terestchenko

10 9 8 7 6 5 4 3 2 1

To Piero and Luca,
who give meaning
to everything

"It was an aesthetic education to live within those walls."

Evelyn Waugh,
BRIDESHEAD REVISITED

Contents

When I was seventeen, and Russia was still the Soviet Union, I took a trip there with my high school. We all went to the Dom Knigi in Leningrad—then, as now, a famous bookstore—and while my friends giggled and bought things by Marx, I rooted around and found an English edition of F. Scott Fitzgerald short stories. It caught my attention because contained in the back was a glossary of Fitzgeraldian terms translated into Russian: "Chicago Beef Princess," "Duesenberg," "champagne cocktail," etc. All the vocabulary that described American high life in the 1920s was explained in little reams of Cyrillic, which I pretended to read with as much interest as "The Diamond as Big as the Ritz." Hanging off of phrases like those, the inscrutable Russian letters and ciphers conjured a sense of atmosphere, and I pictured all the gray Soviet citizens themselves trying to picture Gatsby's blue gardens. Literature is a wonderful way to add layers to something you may think you have finished looking at.

Novel Interiors is a very well-conceived and intimate book that provides a way to build on my experience without having to learn Russian. Lisa Borgnes Giramonti, who loves books and stylish living in no particular order, has discovered a structure for looking at interiors—and for helping you create your own—that is like an invitation to a party. As in the film *Midnight in Paris*, all your favorite writers are there, from whom Lisa has gathered passages and married them to Ivan Terestchenko's beautiful photography. It's hard to say which came first.

The text doesn't offer straight description but more a way to think about *possibilities* in decorating; what things can mean if you do this and then next to it do that. It is user-friendly and meant to be used, because Lisa is generous and a natural hostess and wants to help you elevate and enrich your personal style.

I know many of the rooms in this book, and can tell you it is a different thing to look at them next to words by Isak Dinesen or Vita Sackville-West than just to be there. Through the lens of the words, one sees new things. You might say "I never thought I could make a room that looks like what so-and-so was describing," but maybe you can—and maybe you will. Or maybe you are already in one.

One of my favorite experiences as a decorator was when a client who deeply loved Old Russia asked me to design a bedroom in which Tolstoy would have felt at home. I told her about my experience with the Fitzgerald book in high school, and how interesting it had been to feel my way along the descriptions anew by seeing what the Russians thought strange or important enough to explain. We used language to design, reading patches of Tolstoy and looking at pictures of his house, and I'm happy to say the room was a success. But I'm glad we did this years ago—before Lisa's splendid, friendly, and original book existed—or I might never have gotten the call.

David Netto
LOS ANGELES 2014

We Don't Just Read a Great Story, We Inhabit It

OPPOSITE A kitchen windowsill is a revolving art gallery for favorite treasures. The chandelier adds a captivating bit of drama.

Who can forget the sleek glamour of Gatsby's glittering mansion at West Egg? Or the snug charms of the Dashwood family's dear little cottage in *Sense and Sensibility*? Or the stylish decadence of Dorian Gray's apartment with its black lacquer furniture and porcelain dragon bowls?

If you're at all like me, it's what happens *between* the plot points of a novel that creates the most indelible impression. Of course the story line is important, but what you really remember are all those tiny details that pull you into beautiful worlds that you hate to leave.

When you are surrounded by your own things, it can be difficult to get perspective, see your spaces objectively, and make important decorating decisions. Knowing what style category you fall into can help you home in on a certain scheme and come up with ideas for refreshing your space. Maybe your possessions don't represent who you are anymore. Or you're entering a brand-new phase in your life—merging collections with a loved one or moving into a new home. The only thing you know for sure is that what you have isn't working. But how do you even know where to begin?

Discover Your Design Style Through the Literary Worlds You Love

This is where great literature can come into play: despite the years—and sometimes centuries—that separate us, classic novels can still give us powerful insights into our own lives. What turns *you* on? A bedroom hung with embroideries and antique textiles like in *Out of Africa?* The bare stone floors and rough-hewn wood chairs of *Wuthering Heights?* The idea of a nightly house tradition, like the six o'clock cocktail tray in *Brideshead Revisited?* Don't underestimate how important these details can be to your life. Happiness has a wonderful way of reverberating outward—when you are surrounded by things that bring you a deep sense of well-being, everyone around you feels better, too.

This book is filled with a vast array of richly detailed fictional worlds—from the homespun comforts of *Cranford* to the Mediterranean cool of *Tender Is the Night*—and renowned photographer Ivan Terestchenko's beautiful images bring these novels stirringly to life in homes that exist today. By taking note of all these decorative touches, you can begin to gravitate to the personal design style that represents *you*.

Classic Novels Contain All the Details for Living a Stylish Life

In the chapters that follow, I'll guide you through the enchanting worlds of more than sixty literary classics and show you how they can inspire your decorating style, the ways in which you relax and entertain, and even the fabrics, textures, and colors you are drawn to. Each chapter focuses on a distinct design aesthetic so that you can decide what you love, what you don't, and learn exactly how to re-create the look in your own home.

• In "Shall I Put the Kettle On?" I'll give you the decorating basics that authors like Charles Dickens, Jane Austen, and Elizabeth Gaskell consider

OPPOSITE Natural materials like wood and leather have a mellow luster that comes alive in the half-light.

essential to a home that's cozy and unpretentious. You'll learn how to create the ultimate reading refuge, how to organize the perfect kitchen pantry, and why threadbare rugs have so much soul.

• If you're more drawn to the refined interiors of Edith Wharton, Evelyn Waugh, or Henry James, then start with "Remembrance of Things Past." In it, you'll discover the visual power of symmetry, why buying gold-rimmed china is something you'll never regret, and how to live like you're in a stately home even if you're in a third-floor walk-up.

• Maybe you favor an unvarnished approach to life like Thomas Hardy, D. H. Lawrence, and Willa Cather. In the "Living au Naturel" chapter, it's all about handmade over man-made. You'll learn why a pared-down room feels sacred, how to keep a neutral room from turning ten shades of blah, and how to set your table for a perfect rustic feast.

Rows of blue-and-white plates festoon a hallway. Wooden lipped edges and a metal wire keep each row firmly in place. OPPOSITE A drinks tray is stocked with ingredients for an instant cocktail. Above, a vintage kitchen scale has a pared-down beauty that still feels modern.

• Perhaps you're like F. Scott Fitzgerald, W. Somerset Maugham, and Beverley Nichols and love sleek interiors, geometric patterns, and lots of white and black. In "Oh, the Glamour of It All," I'll explain why reflective surfaces add sophistication to a space, what a great room has in common with a well-tailored wardrobe, and how to set up a classic cordial bar for your next cocktail party.

• Do you embrace color, chaos, and the unconventional? You're in good company—so do Isak Dinesen, Katherine Mansfield, and Lawrence Durrell. In the "Anything Goes" chapter, you'll learn how to mix patterns like a pro, how to re-create some of Virginia Woolf's favorite flower arrangements, and why floor cushions are an absolute must for your home.

• If you appreciate drama in your interiors, chances are you have a little pleasure seeker in you. Head straight to the "Sometimes a Fantasy" chapter and take a cue from authors like Oscar Wilde, Marcel Proust, and Ronald

Firbank. Here, you'll discover the genius of a draped wall, how to add some theatricality to your dinner table, and ways to turn a bedroom into one that's totally Proust-worthy.

Remember, we're all a bit of everything—chances are you have a little bohemian spirit in you even if you prefer the underpinnings of a traditionalist style. Knowing what other design elements appeal to you is a great way to reinvigorate your interiors, to spot what new (or new-to-you) items to bring home, and create a nicely layered home that speaks to who you really are.

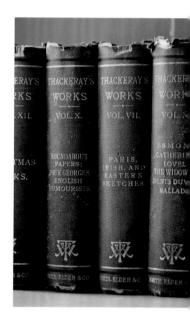

If I Didn't Choose Your Favorite Novel

With a subject of such magnitude, it's inevitable that I may have overlooked one of your favorite novels, and for that I apologize. I had two highly subjective criteria for the books that do appear in these pages. One, they needed to clearly illustrate the major decorating styles and domestic philosophies of each chapter. And two, I mostly restricted my choices to novels that exuded a spirit of good living, or what author Sybille Bedford calls "being *en fête*, of sharing the pleasure of the moment."

The real-life homes in this book, though each unique, share a few important characteristics: they're spirited, they're secure in their skin, and they exude an easy confidence that's irresistible. It's my fervent hope that within these pages you'll find all the decorative inspiration you need to create a personal and stylish environment of your very own.

Wishing you a chic literary journey,
xo, Lisa

OPPOSITE A room layered in a variety of textiles and patterns achieves a look much bigger than the sum of its parts. The solid-colored sofa is key—it anchors the exuberance around it.

Shall I Put the Kettle On?

In the classic novels of Jane Austen, Charles Dickens, George Eliot, and others, home sweet home is a well-worn sanctuary where the furniture is a bit threadbare, the kitchen has yet to be tidied up from breakfast, and a cheerful domesticity reigns over all. Woven into the architecture of these richly detailed worlds are countless lessons on how to live simply and meaningfully. When in doubt, keep it comfortable, they tell us. Embrace the charms of disorder. Go ahead and let the stitches show. And don't ever underestimate the restorative power of a good armchair.

"The Cottage of content [is] better than the Palace of cold splendor, and that was where love was, all was."

Charles Dickens,
DAVID COPPERFIELD

"The hall at Charbury was the most lived-in room of the house. You came into it through the narrow lobby where the hats and coats and walking-sticks were."

Monica Dickens,
MARIANA

These Rooms Are Allowed to Live, Love, and Show Their Laugh Lines

At its most basic, home is a refuge. It's the place where you go to be yourself. If you're always worrying about scratches and spills, how does that enhance your ability to relax and unwind? Or to invite people over, for that matter? Patina is what gives our possessions—and ourselves—character and meaning. Behind every chip and scratch is a story; in *Persuasion*, Jane Austen confirms this when she writes affectionately of a pretty little drawing-room whose faded sofa is a living testament to "four summers and two children."

Divided cubbies provide ample space for shoes underneath. Straw baskets keep everyone in the family organized. **OPPOSITE** Mismatched chairs and plywood wine crates enhance this dining room's cottage feel.

"It was just what it ought to be, and it looked what it was."

Jane Austen,
EMMA

Part of what makes this chair charming is its decrepitude: the tattered fabric alludes to a lively life. OPPOSITE This much-loved sofa has achieved the perfect stage of comfort.

Well-worn furniture feels like an old friend—it knows what position you like to curl up in and exactly where your neck feels most comfortable. In her wonderful novel *Mariana*, Monica Dickens writes about a roomful of arm-chairs "whose springs were at the perfect stage of comfort—half-way between newness and decadence." When it comes to dining tables, a wooden one that's already scarred from a generation of meals takes the stress level way down— who's going to notice one more scratch?

Tattered rugs add texture, patina, and history to any space. In his novels, Charles Dickens mentions a well-worn Turkish carpet or hearth rug as code whenever he wants to indicate a room that's full of soul.

"Although a room of modest situation . . . and of no pretensions to velvet, satin, or gilding, it had got itself established in a domestic position analogous to that of an easy dressing-gown or pair of slippers."

Charles Dickens, OUR MUTUAL FRIEND

Fabric curtains on the lower half of this breakfront cabinet let you display what you like and keep the rest hidden.

"Dinner was nearly ready in
the kitchen—for so I suppose
the room ought to be called,
as there were oak dressers and
cupboards all round."

Elizabeth Gaskell, CRANFORD

OPPOSITE In this cream-paneled pantry, deep shelves hold kitchen essentials at the ready.

A well-stocked pantry quickens both your appetite and your heart. In Charles Dickens's *Our Mutual Friend*, Eugene Wrayburn extols the merits of his: "See! Miniature flour-barrel, rolling-pin, spice-box, shelf of brown jars, chopping-board, coffee-mill . . . The moral influence of these objects, in forming the domestic virtues, may have an immense influence upon me." Whether your pantry is a former utility closet, a kitchen cabinet, or just a few dedicated rows of open shelving, painting it a pretty color, trimming the shelves with brass tacks and grosgrain ribbon, or keeping a few of your favorite cookbooks on display will inspire you to make something delicious every time you gaze at it. It's also a good idea to keep a few provisions on hand in case you find yourself entertaining unexpected guests: roasted nuts have a long shelf life, and an unconventional flavored syrup, like elderflower or black currant, can be mixed with sparkling water and a spirit for an instant cocktail.

A LESSON FROM THE BOOKS

THE VIRTUOUS PANTRY

"'Don't let us make it tidy,' said Mary anxiously. 'It wouldn't be a secret garden if it was tidy.'"

Frances Hodgson Burnett,
THE SECRET GARDEN

A flowering bush presses up against a window and offers a tempting view to inhabitants. **OPPOSITE** An exuberant hedge frames the windows of a bedroom and makes an urban cottage feel like an Arcadian retreat.

A door or window that's clustered round with flowering vines can turn an ordinary view into a magical frame. In Elizabeth Gaskell's *North and South*, "the little casement window in Margaret's bed-chamber was almost filled up with rose and vine branches." There's a liberating beauty to things allowed to grow according to their natural wont . . . and perhaps an inspirational message, too.

Beauty Is Found in Simple Things

A round table stacked with books, a hot supper on a clean tablecloth, a pretty work basket, a jug of wildflowers—authors like Jane Austen and Anthony Trollope believed things like this went a long way in making our environments feel safe, reassuring, and familiar. In *Mariana*, Monica Dickens describes the essence of a house through its scents: "It was the smell of clean sheets that reminded Mary of what . . . she called the Charbury Smell . . . an indefinable pot-pourri of all the fragrant things in the house—roses, wood-smoke, polished floors, bread, and lavender-kept old linen."

Oatmeal-colored linen has an old-school cool to it that's borne out by tradition: in *Lark Rise to Candleford*, Flora Thompson's semiautobiographical novel about a small nineteenth-century English village, the families eat dinner every night on a "table spread with a clean whitey-brown cloth." Flax, the raw mate-

A bowl of antique dice affirms Anthony Trollope's belief that old objects have more soul than new ones. **OPPOSITE** Tongue-in-cheek watercolors reflect an owner's love for vintage Penguin Classics. An antique glass-fronted cabinet displays a fresh stack of bath towels.

"It was a picture of comfort, full of easy-chairs, cushions, and footstools, worked by his mother's hand, and with no sort of thing omitted that could help to render it complete."

Charles Dickens,
DAVID COPPERFIELD

In *David Copperfield*, Charles Dickens writes of a room that's "half parlor and half kitchen." If yours also serves dual purposes, patterned tiles on the floor are an effective way to define a room's cooking and dining areas.

"Out came the four little work-baskets, and the needles flew."

Louisa May Alcott,
LITTLE WOMEN

Framed with love: a needlework owl is a handmade connection to family and adds warmth and history to a room. **OPPOSITE** This snug sleeping refuge, replete with its own bookshelf, built-in drawers, and ship's buoy, reminds me of Peggotty's houseboat in *David Copperfield*.

rial for linen, is durable yet pliant, so its fabric will last for years and gradually become softer every time you wash it.

Plain white cotton sheets have a simple, honest appeal to them that makes going to sleep feel like a personal reward. It's luxury at its most basic and elemental. For the softest sheets, look for a high thread count, but also consider the quality of the thread: luxury weaves like pima, Supima, and Egyptian cotton come from plants with extra-long, silky fibers.

Needlework forges a handmade connection to the past and to the long-standing traditions of domestic life. Old samplers, embroidered cushions, and knitted tea cozies add warmth and history to a room and give people a deeper glimpse into your personal sensibilities. When it comes to framing a vintage piece, try floating or pinning it onto a white mat in a white shadow box (so it can really pop), or even hanging it from the wall in a wooden embroidery hoop.

"The linen . . . though coarse,
was clean and smelt beautifully
of lavender."

Kenneth Grahame,
THE WIND IN THE WILLOWS

A little wooden bridge gives a path leading to a backyard art studio a pastoral charm. **OPPOSITE** This wooden covered gate welcomes visitors in laid-back style and would make a perfect arbor for climbing roses.

A colorful front door, an amusing knocker, a few tubs of flowering plants, an iron boot scraper shaped like an animal, or a generously sized doormat will establish a cheerful stance before guests even cross the threshold. In *Emma*, Jane Austen writes of Emma's delight in passing a cottage one morning: "Oh, what a sweet house! There are the yellow curtains that Miss Nash admires so much." If you want to take charm to the next level, think up a name for your house and engrave it on a plaque beside the front door.

A LESSON FROM THE BOOKS
NAMING YOUR HOUSE

Giving your house a name sets a lighthearted tone and invests it with a bit of character. There are many different ways to choose a name—maybe it describes a particular feature of your property, such as its landscape or location (Hilltop or Shady Rest, for example), hints at an amusing quirk or attribute (Five Corners), alludes to a bygone time (Arcadia), or even represents the style of those who live within it (Bedlam). Below, a few celebrated literary examples.

BARTON COTTAGE
(Sense and Sensibility)

HARTFIELD
(Emma)

MOLE END and
TOAD HALL
(The Wind in the Willows)

THE SMALL HOUSE
AT ALLINGTON
(the Barsetshire novels)

HOWARDS END
(Howards End)

THE ROOKERY
(David Copperfield)

PLUMSTEAD
(The Warden)

THRUSHCROSS GRANGE
(Wuthering Heights)

Cheerful touches like a blue door, some
irrepressible flowering bushes, and a
meandering stone path give this cottage
an entrance to remember.

"There's the tulips on the cups, and the roses, as anybody might go and look at 'em for pleasure."

George Eliot,
THE MILL ON THE
FLOSS

OPPOSITE A beautifully worn butcher-block counter does double duty as spice repository and work space.

Purpose Is More Important Than Pedigree

It doesn't matter where the furniture comes from as long as it makes you feel good. An old flea-market sofa that still supports hours of literary wanderings has a value that makes it all the dearer. Its usefulness, not its bloodline, is what counts—no matter how humble its origins, an object that serves a role radiates its own nobility.

A collection of mismatched china for everyday use has a nonchalance to it that's both liberating and creative. Flora Thompson gives the classic blue-and-white version a shout-out in *Lark Rise to Candleford*—"A blue-and-white dish of oranges stuck with cloves stood on the dresser"—but all patterns and colors are equally welcome in this unpretentious style. The idea is to keep everything fairly inexpensive, so if a piece accidentally falls short of the kitchen counter, it's not a calamity, merely an opportunity to embark on an interesting new treasure hunt.

"It was indeed very compact
and comfortable . . . [with]
pots, pans, jugs and kettles of
every size and variety."

Kenneth Grahame,
THE WIND IN THE WILLOWS

COLLECTING DINING CHAIRS

A great dinner party is one where each guest's personality is allowed to shine, so why shouldn't the same principle apply to your dining chairs? If you've always been attracted to the laid-back vibe of a mismatched set, keep a few tips in mind to make sure everything looks good.

- To start with, all seat heights should be approximately the same so that everyone sits at approximately the same height.

- Keep an eye on balance: if your side chairs are mismatched, try anchoring the heads of the table with two of the same armchair.

- Finally, make sure there's at least one common denominator. Maybe you paint all the chairs the same color or upholster them in the same fabric. Or maybe they're all made of wood, metal, or plastic. Either way, they'll share a similarity and still celebrate their differences.

OPPOSITE Dark paneling gives a dining room a snug feeling, and the wallpaper is a cheeky solution for a room not big enough for bookshelves.

"The people whom she had hitherto known just put what they had or could get into their homes, old things and new things, side by side with each other."

Flora Thompson,
LARK RISE TO CANDLEFORD

"Everything was old, venerable, and picturesque. . . . The dining-room [was] paneled with black wainscoting."

Anthony Trollope, ORLEY FARM

Every Room Feels as Cozy and Welcoming as the Kitchen

Have you ever wondered why at a party everyone ends up congregating in the kitchen? If you ask me, it's because the kitchen is usually the least pretentious room in the house. It's not out to prove anything, and it doesn't sit in judgment of anyone—after all, its fundamental purpose is to serve. In a kitchen, conversation gets looser, laughter gets louder, and if you knock something over, well, it's probably not the first time that's happened. (Revelation: an accident is an unscheduled opportunity to make your guests feel more comfortable.) A home that embraces these qualities is a place friends will return to again and again.

Mug hooks, vintage tins, antique drawer pulls, and pleasingly arranged stacks of dishes turn this antique cabinet into a bespoke mini-larder. **OPPOSITE** With a marble top added to it, an antique table offers versatility for baking and cooking.

"She has the idea that one night in your house would give her pleasure and do her good. . . . Being one of those imaginative girls, the presence of all our books and furniture soothes her."

E. M. Forster,
HOWARDS END

The friendliest homes seem to have an untidiness that enhances their beauty, with books crammed into the recesses, flowers trailing around the windows, and half-completed projects scattered on the dining room table. In Louisa May Alcott's *Little Women*, there's a blissful-sounding "wilderness of books" in the March family's library that Jo hurries to every chance she can.

A good armchair is a private little piece of real estate. Curling up in one is like getting an upholstered hug: it enfolds you and offers a snug retreat from the world beyond. In Elizabeth Gaskell's novel *Cranford*, a well-worn chintz easy chair is Miss Matty's throne of choice in the evenings. And don't understate the importance of armrests. There are those who say home is where you hang your hat, but personally, I think it's where you rest your elbows.

OPPOSITE Here, well-worn furniture, faded rugs, and details like knitted throws, old books, and treasured mementoes liberate a room from stuffiness.

"When they got home, the Rat
made a bright fire in the parlor,
and planted the Mole in an
armchair in front of it."

Kenneth Grahame,
THE WIND IN THE WILLOWS

This grandfather clock and the little wooden dog perched on it are a tender tribute to faithful companions. **OPPOSITE** An old leather armchair, a tattered rug, a pile of books, and a crackling fire transform a Hollywood bedroom into a cozy English scene.

CREATING THE ULTIMATE COZY CORNER

A warm and inviting nook can make the difference between a room you merely pass through and one you actually spend time in. Here, tips for creating your own little refuge.

- *Choose a corner that's out of the way of foot traffic.* You want to create a space where you'll be able to get in some uninterrupted time for reading or relaxing.

- *Find a space near a window.* The serenity of natural light and a cool breeze can never be undervalued. If you don't have a convenient window, though, don't worry. A plant or small tree nearby can give you the same sense of the great outdoors.

- *The right seating is crucial.* I'm partial to a roomy armchair with a seat that's fairly low to the ground. If you're going to be spending a lot of time here, make sure the incline and curvature of the chair work with your body. A longer seat depth of 38 to 43 inches will give you room enough to put your knees up should you wish.

- *A footstool or an ottoman will create extra legroom.* You can always match the fabric to the chair—it will visually elongate it and make the seating look more like a chaise—but upholstering it in a coordinating color looks just as nice. Or try a vintage leather ottoman, which goes with pretty much everything.

- *Choose a pillow that's 12 inches by 18 inches* to work equally well as lumbar support, headrest, and elbow propper. I have a velvet one that I filled loosely with a mixture of dried lavender and buckwheat hulls, and every time I smush it into a new shape, it gives off the most amazing scent.

- *A small end table nearby will give you someplace to set a drink;* a basket will make a convenient catchall for reading material; and a small tray or box— John Derian makes nice ones—that holds reading glasses, notepads, and pencils will keep you nicely organized.

- *Finally, bring in the details.* Flowers, candles (amber-scented ones smell like an old house), a lap blanket, and a pair of cozy slippers are a few sybaritic extras that will keep you firmly planted there.

OPPOSITE Then there was light: a well-placed reading lamp ensures that a cozy armchair is an illuminating refuge to curl up in.

"Jo hurried to this quiet place,
and curling herself up in the
easy chair, devoured poetry,
romance, history, travels,
and pictures like a regular
bookworm."

Louisa May Alcott,
LITTLE WOMEN

This petite snuggery has a reassuring security that a larger room can sometimes lack. Warm brown walls intensify the charm. **OPPOSITE** An upholstered L-shaped banquette creates a cozy kitchen nook and does double duty as a homework command post.

Small rooms grant a quiet power to their inhabitants, perhaps because they offer an intimacy that doesn't intimidate or overwhelm (as a larger room can). In *Our Mutual Friend*, the cozy proportions of Mr. Boffin's room are much prized: "Far less grand than the rest of the house, it was far more comfortable, being pervaded by a certain air of homely snugness." A little peace and quiet, and a little space—sometimes isn't that all a home needs?

"The place had certainly the
appearance of warmth and life
which comes from frequent use."

Anthony Trollope, ORLEY FARM

"In every nook and corner there was some queer little table, or cupboard, or bookcase, or seat, or something or other, that made me think there was not such another good corner in the room; until I looked at the next one, and found it equal to it, if not better."

Charles Dickens, DAVID COPPERFIELD

"Simple elegance is what
we aim at . . . make
it all look pretty, and
impromptu, and natural."

Elizabeth Gaskell,
WIVES AND
DAUGHTERS

The Finishing Touches

Look for these items the next time you find yourself wanting to add a little rosy domestic glow to your home.

Tea accessories (kettles, tea canisters, trays, Brown Betty teapots, wooden tea chests)

Brightly colored crockery

Vintage metal tins

Brass candlestick holders

Lattice trellis or fencing for garden landscaping

Framed animal portraits

Cracked leather ottomans

Beeswax candles

Peg shelving

Rush matting

Iron strap hinges for cabinetry

Toby jug figurines

Sunderland lustreware

China cake stands

Rag rugs

Wooden plate racks

Tartan blankets

Ceramic water jugs and basins

Small round mirrors

Swiss cuckoo clocks

Mason Cash mixing bowls

Punch bowls

Iron bedsteads

Vintage breadboards

Hot-water bottles with knitted covers

Cast-iron animal boot scrapers

Wainscot paneling

A repainted breakfront cabinet makes a lovely destination for flea market treasures. **OPPOSITE** A hand-stitched sampler by Reed van Brunschot tells visitors exactly what the owner holds dear.

" If people do but know how to set about it, every comfort may be as well enjoyed in a cottage as in the most spacious dwelling."

Jane Austen, **SENSE AND SENSIBILITY**

Ample seating, a table piled with books and flowers, and colorful landscapes framed in wood give this room a bright, relaxed feel.

Remembrance of Things Past

Some homes feel so immediately reassuring and hospitable when you walk into them that you can't help but exhale. Think of Evelyn Waugh's fictional Brideshead, or the classic stately homes described in novels by Edith Wharton and Henry James: these interiors radiate ease in spite of their formal elegance—or possibly because of it. Such houses were at one time run like small hotels by a full-time staff whose job it was to anticipate every desire and triple-check every detail. Few of us live like that anymore, but what's significant about the interiors described in this chapter is not so much their lavishness but the graciousness that informs them. Harmony equals elegance, these authors confide to us. Rituals and traditions keep history alive. Discretion is everything. Call it understated luxury— it's that little bit less that adds up to a whole lot more.

"A certain fashion of expensive simplicity
was beginning to make itself felt; a certain
taste was arising, which tended to eliminate
unnecessary objects."

Vita Sackville-West, THE EDWARDIANS

"At Brideshead they used small individual spirit decanters which . . . were placed before anyone who asked for it."

Evelyn Waugh,
BRIDESHEAD
REVISITED

Rooms Are Designed to Whisper, Not Shout

Serene color palettes emanate a sweet-tempered restraint that encourages mental repose and is anything but showy. A room decorated in "all gentle curves and light colors" like the one Thomas Mann describes in his novel *Buddenbrooks* makes you want to linger in it. Dark hues can have a similar effect—a study with deep-toned walls and coordinating fabrics and patterns has a calming richness that echoes outward.

When it comes to versatility, tufted upholstery is an elegant workhorse. Besides evincing a classic buttoned-up look, a tufted sofa, chair, or ottoman is low-maintenance—it has no loose cushions that require constant fluffing or

Individual glass decanters serve as a chic solution for guests with different beverage preferences. **OPPOSITE** The strong, classic stripes on this sofa act as a grounding force for the trio of artworks hanging above it.

Low tufted chairs have a
welcoming air that begs you to
sink down into them. **OPPOSITE**
A recessed nook in the rear of a
living room provides an intimate
refuge for reading and tête-à-
tête conversations.

straightening. Furniture like this is also incredibly comfortable; in *Vanity Fair,*
William Thackeray describes a character's encounter with one of these honor-
able creatures: "She sank back into [the chair's] arms as if it were an old friend."
Another benefit of tufting is longevity—reinforcing the fabric every few inches
keeps it from sagging and wearing unevenly.

Gold-rimmed china is one of those purchases you'll never regret: it's understated and timeless and goes with everything. In British novelist Henry Green's
classic *Loving,* the butler, Raunce, brazenly drinks his afternoon tea out of his

"The furnishings were all gentle curves and light colors."

Thomas Mann,
BUDDENBROOKS

Clean lines, pale colors, and strong symmetry give this living room an airy spaciousness that belies the amount of furniture in it.

master's heirloom cup and saucer, a small but telling example of how fine china shouldn't be reserved for special occasions. Nighttime allows dishes like this to really come into their own, though—under candlelight, those gold rims take on an enchanting gleam. Look for the classic brands like Royal Worcester, Meissen, Limoges, Royal Copenhagen, and Rosenthal.

Chintz and stripes have been hanging out together for centuries, and for good reason: the feminine sensibility of a printed floral fabric paired with a bold graphic stripe results in a visual tension—delicate meets strong, linear meets curved—that never ceases to appeal. In Julia Strachey's *Cheerful Weather for the Wedding*, the stripes are no less dramatic for being heaven-sent: "Sunlight fell in dazzling oblongs through the windows upon the faded wisteria on the cretonne sofas and armchairs."

Gold-rimmed china is eternally chic and takes on an enchanting gleam under candlelight. **OPPOSITE** Breakfast essentials set out on a countertop or kitchen island allow houseguests to help themselves and hosts to get on with their day.

The Past Has One Foot Firmly Rooted in the Present

Although checkerboard floors date to Roman times, today they more often evoke the splendor of stately European homes. In Henry Green's *Loving*, there's a marble checkerboard floor in the entry hall as well as a luxe carpeted version in Lady Tennant's bedroom. The simple graphic pattern of a checkerboard makes it especially suited to public spaces like foyers and kitchens, but it can be just as effective in more private areas like bathrooms, and in materials like flagstone, tile, and ceramic.

Baronial details conjure up historical mystique and are a tangible link to the splendors of the past. Objects like medieval brass rubbings, lion-head door knockers, and heraldic coats of arms add patina and character to a room that's only one layer deep. Their very presence is a nod to tradition and to "catching and keeping the best of each generation," as Evelyn Waugh described it.

A cement checkerboard floor and gleaming range tucked into an alcove are a modern take on the manor house kitchen hearth. **OPPOSITE** Air plants mounted on wooden boards echo the stag antlers mentioned in novels such as *The Edwardians* and *Brideshead Revisited*.

"The hall was large and high, with a flagged floor; . . . antlers full of stags ornamented the walls, opposite the full-length Van Dycks."

Vita Sackville-West,
THE EDWARDIANS

"On each side of the shiny painted steps was a large
blue china flower-pot on a bright yellow china stand."

Edith Wharton, THE AGE OF INNOCENCE

Treasure chest: Abandoned birds' nests, each with a little gold egg inside, become steeped in mystery when displayed in a vintage commode. **OPPOSITE** Staggered shelving sets the stage for a captivating collection of natural ephemera. **PREVIOUS PAGES** Stone urns flank a doorway and invest an entry hall with a bit of baronial grandeur. A grassy lawn offers a horticultural spin on the traditional checkerboard floor.

When it comes to bibelots, or decorative accessories, there's a delicate line between order and clutter. Instead of displaying little treasures everywhere, gather them together on one or two tabletops—not only will this give them the feel of a collection, but it also keeps other surfaces free for guests to use. In Evelyn Waugh's *Brideshead Revisited,* Lady Marchmain uses her chimneypiece as a destination for her small treasures.

In the nineteenth century, traveling across Europe was a vital part of an upper-class education. Travelers came home with their heads spinning and their suitcases bursting with trophies like Egyptian obelisks, Greek busts, miniature Roman temples, English prints, and French campaign tables, which wound up in stately homes everywhere. The house in *Brideshead Revisited* is filled with treasures collected by the Marchmain family; from Daumier etchings and views of Florence to Sèvres vases and an entire room devoted to Pompeii, it reverberates with the grace and elegance of centuries past.

GRAND TOUR MEMENTOS

Rooms Are Designed with Order and Purpose in Mind

We have an inherent predisposition toward visual harmony. Rooms with a strong sense of balance and order tell our brains to relax. If your architecture isn't symmetrical, a pair of objects flanking a focal point like a door, hallway, or fireplace will make a room feel more harmonious. Objects don't have to match, either—as long as they're similar, they'll still provide that sense of rest that the eye is looking for.

Upholstered doors have a practical chic to them: they muffle sound and can transform a ho-hum swing door between a kitchen and dining room into one fit for the chicest of parties. In *Brideshead Revisited*, Sebastian Flyte takes Charles Ryder on a tour to the servants' quarters "through a baize door into a dark corridor." Baize, a dense woolen fabric similar to that used for billiard tables, was a typical covering for nineteenth-century upholstered doors, but today leather—or faux leather—is more practical, and it looks even better cracked and aged.

Stacked wicker baskets from IKEA offer a clever twist on storage. The contents of each are written on luggage tags. **OPPOSITE** Open sesame: a jib door paneled and upholstered to match the wall surrounding it leads to a secret library.

Designed to accommodate all kinds of
activities and moods, this living room
exemplifies the ones in Edith Wharton's
The Age of Innocence with "deep curtained
windows and comfortable sofas."

A portiere is a curtain or heavy drape traditionally hung over a doorway to keep the heat of a fireplace in and fierce winds at bay. But portieres have a decorative purpose as well. Draping a passageway adds drama and mystery—when you hide something from view, you arouse a curiosity that begs to be satisfied. Here are a few more tips.

- *Use portieres to define spaces.* If you live in a loft and find yourself craving more solitude, dividing a large area with a curtain can create two distinct rooms out of one. Line each side with a different fabric to give each room a distinctly different atmosphere.

- *Hang a portiere in unexpected places:* between your living room and dining room, at the end of a long hall to create a focal point, or even in front of a windowed sitting area for a private reading nook.

- *Draping adds layers of softness to a room,* perfect if the proportions of your living space are stiff or boxy. Allowing the curtain panels to pool one to three inches on the floor gives a relaxed look that still feels tailored—any longer than that and they'll need readjusting every time you open or close them.

- *Installing a portiere a few inches above the door opening* rather than inside the doorjamb adds visual height to a room.

- *In a standard-sized doorway, hang a single panel of fabric* and then tie it to one side with a tieback. A wide passageway (such as sliding doors that open into two rooms) requires at least two fabric panels, one on each side of the doorway.

- *For a tieback, traditional options include passementerie,* ribbon, bullion fringe, or the same fabric as the curtain. Or go for something more personalized, like a velvet rope in a contrasting color.

- *In the fall and winter, choose a fabric that's sensuous and thick like velvet* or damask (and add a lining to reduce drafts). In the summer, switch it out for something light and airy, like a striped muslin, a printed Indian cotton, or a sexy sheer organza.

ADD DRAMA WITH PORTIERES

"Directly opposite, portieres of some green fabric had been pulled back to reveal the brown silk salon and a tall glass door."

Thomas Mann,
BUDDENBROOKS

"It was an aesthetic education to live within those walls, to wander from room to room, from the Soanesque library to the Chinese drawing-room, adazzle with gilt pagodas and nodding mandarins, painted paper and Chippendale fret-work."

Evelyn Waugh,
BRIDESHEAD REVISITED

The hand-painted Gracie Studio wallpaper and collection of Chinese ginger jars could come straight from the pages of *Brideshead Revisited*. **OPPOSITE** A blue-and-white porcelain bowl and scenic wallpaper by Zuber et Cie bring drama to a dining room.

Distant Climes Beckon

Chinoiserie—the French word for "Chinese-esque"—embraces the romance of the Far East and adds exoticism to a room. Asian-inspired fabrics and wallpapers emblazoned with birds and flowering branches are a chief hallmark of this ornate style, but patterned garden stools and blue-and-white porcelain ginger jars are also easy ways to make your own chinoiserie statement.

You don't need a massive indoor conservatory like the one in Thomas Mann's *Buddenbrooks* to create your own little garden paradise. In Edith Wharton's *The Age of Innocence*, New York's fashionable society cultivates ferns in Wardian cases, those miniature iron and glass houses that you can find in upscale garden shops. If the graceful maidenhair ferns so popular in turn-of-the-century novels aren't your cup of tea, try decorating with sculptural plants like succulents, fiddle-leaf figs, and topiaries—they'll add structure to a room without taking it over.

A leafy fern is part of a trio of decorative objects that echo the angle of a staircase. **OPPOSITE** Dark windows and a red-brick floor give this garden room the atmosphere of a traditional nineteenth-century orangery.

"More even than the work of the great architects, I loved buildings that grew silently with the centuries, catching and keeping the best of each generation."

Evelyn Waugh,
BRIDESHEAD REVISITED

Cane, wicker, and bamboo have been a hit with the beau monde going back to the days of pharaohs and emperors. Its weather-resistant qualities, high strength-to-weight ratio, and slender profile make it a practical and chic choice for portable furniture: in her novel *The Edwardians*, Vita Sackville-West writes of wicker furniture on the lawn during an outdoor house party at the fictional Chevron.

A mirrored wall doubles a bathroom's luxury appeal. Cashmere curtains complete the fantasy. OPPOSITE A wicker chair's golden hue reappears in a library's bamboo blinds. White-spined design magazines blend unobtrusively into bookshelves.

A Home Should Mirror the Graciousness of Its Owners

A monogram can turn an ordinary household object into an heirloom. Traditionally used to make sure Lord So-and-So's nightshirt didn't end up on his guest's torso, today monograms add a personal touch to headboards, cushions, chair covers, and even lampshades. Whether you choose to emblazon them in a contrasting color or keep them subtly tone-on-tone is up to you: in *The Edwardians*, a guest room at Chevron has monogrammed bedsheets that are visible only once you turn down the counterpane.

Adding monograms to towels or bed linens is a small detail that leaves a lasting impression. **OPPOSITE** Decor books stacked below an elegant cocktail table make clever use of free space.

You don't need to live in a stately home to enjoy the benefits of centuries of tradition. Little domestic rituals have meaning that goes beyond appearance; they forge a link to the past and act as an emotional buoy in today's rapidly changing world. Here are a few customs worth keeping alive.

- *Invest in a few glass wine decanters, and then use them*—both when guests visit and for a weeknight dinner. (They do no one any good in the back of that cabinet.) In *Brideshead Revisited*, small individual decanters are placed in front of each guest at dinnertime.

- *Have a set of house stationery printed up* like the Duchess of Chevron does in *The Edwardians* and use it for multiple occasions: as invitations to dinner parties, for thank-you notes, and for leaving in guests' rooms.

- *If hosting family over the holidays, set up a simple breakfast bar* so you're free to get on with your day and others can help themselves. For a guest, this kind of approach is so much more relaxing than having someone hover over you for your order.

- *Air out your sheets every day.* When you get up in the morning, toss back the bedcovers and, if possible, open the windows—even fifteen minutes is time enough to reinvigorate your sheets and help them last longer between washings.

- *"Put out a handkerchief dipped in eau de cologne."* This tip comes straight from the pages of *The Edwardians*, and there's something wonderfully stimulating about a scented room provided it's done with a light hand. Spritz a few drops of perfume on a pillow or favorite chair. Or try a luxury room spray—they're specially formulated not to overwhelm the senses.

"Wood must be cut and carried, hot-water bottles put into beds, inkstands filled, breakfast trays prepared, blinds raised or lowered . . . life . . . must be made as pleasant as possible."

Vita Sackville-West,
THE EDWARDIANS

"There were objects of every sort [on the table]—made of porcelain, nickel, silver and gold, of wood, silk, and linen."

Thomas Mann, BUDDENBROOKS

By pairing objects with similar sensibilities from vastly different time periods, you call attention to what's changed and what's remained the same. **OPPOSITE** A center hall table and a goat-hoofed bench by Myra Hoefer are the elegant stars of an entry foyer.

The Finishing Touches

Seeking to add a sense of tradition and graciousness to your home? Look out for these "remnants of the past" the next time you go shopping.

Fireplace fenders	Sundials	Dark woodwork
Silhouette portraits	Three-branched candlesticks	Valet trays
Garden urns and statuary	Ginger jars	Tassels and fringe
Pineapple accents	Old Master prints	Leaf prints
Antiquarian maps	Bamboo jardinières	Staffordshire ceramic dogs
Old war medals	Paintings of hunting scenes	Old silver trophies
Celadon and jade bowls	Antique brass fittings	Shagreen boxes
Ormolu	Finial-topped chairs	Soup terrines
Agate-handled paper knives	Days of the Raj–inspired items	Glass globe paperweights
Velvet fringed tablecloths		

" That was the story told
by ever so many things in
the house, which betrayed
the full perception of a
comfortable, liberal, deeply
domestic effect, addressed
to eternities of possession. "

Henry James, **A LONDON LIFE**

Living au Naturel

For Emily Brontë, D. H. Lawrence, Willa Cather, and others, everything important begins with the earth. The domestic interiors in their novels resonate with us because they so powerfully embody the values of the landscape around them. These novels show us that by peeling back the layers, we can live simply and authentically. Case in point: in the stark moors of Emily Brontë's *Wuthering Heights* we grasp the spiritual beauty of a minimally furnished home. In the description of Thomas Hardy's gray Wessex twilight we surrender to the allure of a tranquil palette. In the rush of pleasure *Anne of Green Gables* gets from an armful of autumn branches, we see the vitality that nature can bestow on a room. Look beyond yourself, these authors urge us. It's only by studying the exterior world that we can discover what makes us truly happy.

"I'm so glad I live in a world where there are Octobers. . . . Look at these maple branches. Don't they give you a thrill— several thrills? I'm going to decorate my room with them."

L. M. Montgomery,
ANNE OF GREEN GABLES

"By doing without many so-called necessities, he had managed to have his luxuries."

Willa Cather,
THE PROFESSOR'S
HOUSE

Austerity Is the Ultimate Sophistication

Henry David Thoreau had it exactly right when he said, "A man is rich in proportion to the number of things he can afford to let alone." For the authors in this chapter, when we whittle down our possessions, what remains becomes more sacred. In *Walden*, Thoreau writes of a house "where you can see all the treasures . . . at one view, and everything hangs upon its peg that a man should use."

There's a serenity to pared-down rooms that comes from the freedom to focus on ideas instead of objects. In his short story "The Captain's Doll," D. H. Lawrence describes a room as being beautiful in part because it has "very little furniture save large peasant cupboards or presses of painted wood, and a huge writing-table." There's nothing more inefficient than a house filled with

A sky-blue landscape adds vibrancy and dimension to a bookshelf. **OPPOSITE** Plain walnut shelves echo the gardener's hut "paneled with unvarnished deal" in *Lady Chatterley's Lover*. **PREVIOUS PAGES** This solid walnut island is a powerful reminder that everything begins with the earth.

> "The ease that belongs to simplicity is charming enough to make up for whatever a simple life may lack."
>
> Sarah Orne Jewett,
> THE COUNTRY OF
> THE POINTED FIRS

Upholstering a daybed by a window in a calm neutral hue ensures that the Hollywood Hills are the star. **OPPOSITE** Above the madding crowd: twig fencing laid across a simple frame gives an outdoor dining area the appeal of a rustic refuge.

things you don't use—although some people may revel in a space that's cluttered, for you it doesn't offer any creative breathing room. Let other people call your rooms plain. To you, they're well edited and all that you could want.

Multipurpose objects allow plenty of room for a more minimal style of living. In D. H. Lawrence's *Sons and Lovers*, there's a trestle table that can easily be moved and taken apart should the area be needed for another activity. A bench that doubles as a seat, a coffee table, and a place to rest your feet is perfect for those looking to emulate the no-frills simplicity of Thoreau's *Walden*. This kind of decorating isn't about following rules; it's about seeing the versatility in everything and never being afraid to improvise.

"The [roof's] entire anatomy [lay]
bare to an inquiring eye."

Emily Brontë,
WUTHERING HEIGHTS

"Majestic without severity, impressive without showiness, [and] grand in its simplicity."

Thomas Hardy,
THE RETURN OF
THE NATIVE

Materials Are Unpretentious and Trend-Resistant

Elements like wood, stone, and clay have a spiritual component that fills a home with nature and, thus, life. In Sarah Orne Jewett's *The Country of Pointed Firs*, the narrator loves to sit in her room "with the brown unpainted paneling of its woodwork." Not for these characters the gleam of a highly polished chandelier. They prefer the dull luster of a terra-cotta bowl or the way the sun's rays reveal the intricate grain of a wooden chair.

Corded walnut chairs give airiness to a dining table and let the view shine through. **OPPOSITE** Practical wooden furniture has a plainspoken honesty that makes it all the more distinctive.

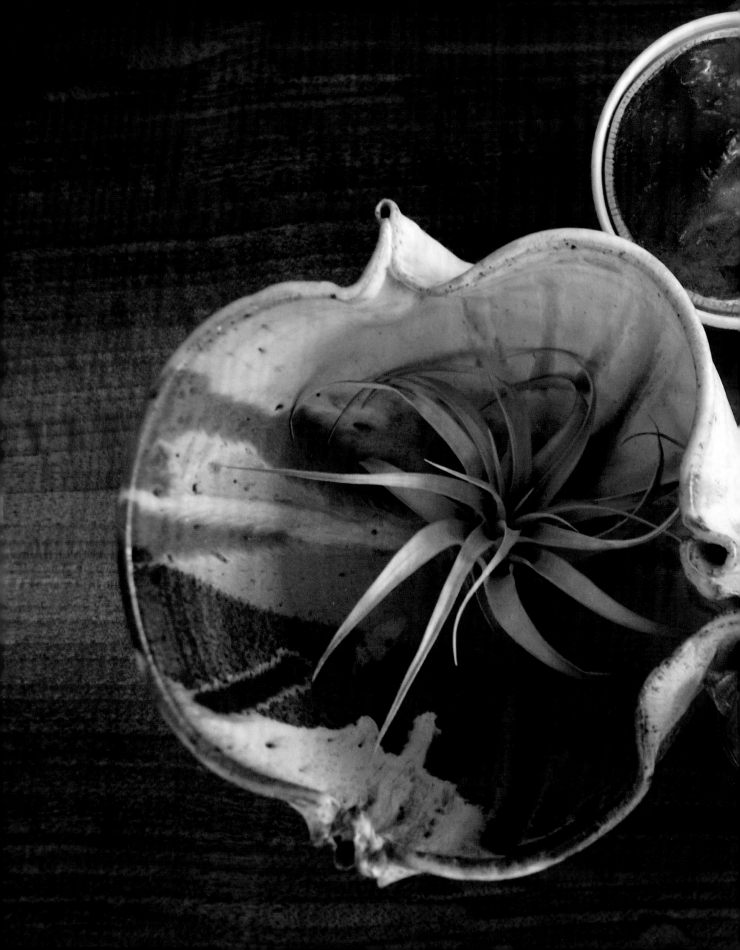

"He was a primitive. . . . He seemed to
be at the root of the matter; Desire
under all desires, Truth under all
Truths. . . . [He] was earth and would
return to earth."

Willa Cather,
THE PROFESSOR'S HOUSE

"Nothing is too small or too trifling to . . . acquire dignity."

Nathaniel Hawthorne, THE SCARLET LETTER

Weathered planks from an outdoor planter have been refashioned into folding doors for a kitchen pass-through. **OPPOSITE** Rustic graffiti: Despite its pop art roots, this Andy Warhol piece totally fits in with the owner's organic aesthetic.

What is it about wood anyway? Thoreau writes about it in *Walden*: "It is remarkable what a value is still put upon [it] even in this age and in this new country, a value more permanent and universal than that of gold." This idea holds just as true today. No other material is so closely intertwined with the culture of humankind—since time immemorial it's warmed us, sheltered us, and comforted us. Every piece tells its own unique story, so before you repaint that battered old dresser, take another look and see if perhaps it's more meaningful left just as it is.

"Anne was curled up Turk-fashion
on the hearth-rug, gazing into that
joyous glow where the sunshine of a
hundred summers was being distilled
from the maple cordwood."

L. M. Montgomery,
ANNE OF GREEN GABLES

Stone is at once ancient and modern, dignified and ordinary. In *Wuthering Heights*, the smooth white stone floors in the manor house lend Heathcliff's rough-hewn furniture—"high-backed, primitive structures"—a sculptural nobility. Stone floors look wonderful in foyers and mudrooms because they forge an instant connection between indoors and outdoors. When it comes to stone countertops, it's worth looking into versions that are honed but left unpolished, like granite or soapstone. They won't remain pristine forever, and that's exactly the point—with time, they'll gain a patina that's rich in personal character.

Accessories can have sacred qualities, too. Classic and unostentatious, earthenware has a mellow glow even under harsh light. Over time it takes on an interesting crackle, or "crazing," and looks even better when passed down from previous generations—a good reason to scour your local antique shops if you don't have access to heirlooms. In *Sons and Lovers*, earthenware is what Mrs. Morel cooks with: "a great bowl of thick red earth." There are many kinds—majolica, faience, and Delft, for example—but creamware, terra-cotta, and Japanese raku ware have an organic lyricism that's more in keeping with this rustic style.

Less is more: A home decorated with a minimal touch gets straight to the heart of the matter. OPPOSITE A wooden altar table, oversized candlesticks, and flowering branches radiate a monastic austerity against a sandstone brick wall.

Enlightenment from on high: a second-story bookcase keeps the lower half of a room uncluttered. **OPPOSITE** Open shelving where you can see all treasures at one view reinforces the credo of owning what you love and using what you have.

"He was rather proud of his home. . . . The chairs were only wooden, and the sofa was old . . . [but] there was a simplicity in everything, and plenty of books."

D. H. Lawrence, SONS AND LOVERS

"He preferred sermons in stones to sermons in churches."

Thomas Hardy,
TESS OF THE
D'URBERVILLES

A gnarled branch of driftwood holds candles and is elevated to sculpture on a sideboard. **OPPOSITE** A repurposed industrial cart holds salvaged treasures and doubles as a potting bench.

Here, the Raw Triumphs Over the Refined

D. H. Lawrence loathed the dehumanizing effects of modern industry and believed man's saving grace was his connection with nature. He describes Lady Chatterley as having the vulnerability of a wildflower: "She wasn't all tough rubber-goods-and-platinum, like the modern girl." Resist the allure of the new and shiny, he tells us. Fancy silver spoons don't make a meal taste more delicious.

Shells and driftwood have a primitive delicacy that lends a lovely grace note to a room. In *The Country of the Pointed Firs*, both of these decorative accessories make an appearance: conch shells brought home from ships' voyages decorate a mantelpiece, and "pieces o' wood and boards that drove ashore" are

collected by villagers and given a second life in their homes. A gnarled piece of driftwood can make a simple but stunning centerpiece for a table, especially when surrounded by votive candles or trailing ivy. Conch shells also make great pot containers for succulents like jade or aloe, and most nurseries will oblige you by drilling a hole in the bottom for drainage.

Raw nubby textures like straw, seagrass, rush, and willow give the eye another decorative layer to feast on—a good way to add visual interest to rooms without adding color. In *Wuthering Heights*, Zillah the housekeeper keeps willow baskets in every room for storing food, firewood, and domestic handiwork. In *The Country of the Pointed Firs*, the villagers sew braided rushes together to make floor mats and thick cushions for a window seat.

Woven baskets layer a room with texture—in *Wuthering Heights*, they're used to store food, firewood, and housekeeping supplies. **OPPOSITE** Seagrass matting, flowering branches, and neutral-hued furniture give this room an elegant rustic appeal.

"[They] lead rich, emotional lives and . . .
live intensely and with a wild poetry."

Stella Gibbons, COLD COMFORT FARM

Beauty lies in the unadorned. There's an appealing candor to plain furniture that was made to perform and not just sit there and look pretty. A sturdy oak table exudes a proletariat strength and simplicity that is key to its raw beauty. In *Sons and Lovers*, D. H. Lawrence writes of a dwelling, "It had been originally a laborer's cottage. And the furniture was old and battered. But Paul loved it." Industrial-style decor is another way of reinforcing this emphasis on function over form—a vintage medical cabinet makes a great liquor bar, for example, and a metal factory stool looks perfectly at home up against a wooden counter.

A LESSON FROM THE BOOKS

SETTING THE RUSTIC TABLE

In *The Country of the Pointed Firs*, Sarah Orne Jewett describes a rustic feast as beautiful as it is delicious. The villagers trim the edges of the tables with oak leaves and gather wildflowers from the field to create random little rustic bouquets. The result is an unpretentious dinner full of grace and gladness. Below, a few ideas on how to set a table that feeds your spirit as well as your stomach.

- *If you don't have a wooden table, cover yours with a length of undyed burlap*—it makes a practical tablecloth for all seasons and looks as appropriate on an outdoor picnic table as it does in the dining room dressed up with bone-handled cutlery and pewter goblets. Buy it by the yard and just cut it to the size you need. Don't worry about hemming it: the frayed edges add texture and a homespun feeling.

- *Instead of plunking down one fancy arrangement in the middle of the table*, take inspiration from a field of wildflowers and group small bunches of blooms intermittently along a table. Or scatter ferns and roses along it like Anne does in *Anne of Green Gables*: "Having . . . a very artistic taste of her own, she made that tea table . . . a thing of beauty."

- *Cream-colored pillar candles have a nice heft to them* and take on pastoral charm when set inside iron hurricane holders.

- *On a buffet table, tie stacks of vintage books together* with jute twine and use them as makeshift food trivets and plate stands.

"As I looked up and down the tables there was a good cheer, a grave soberness that shone with pleasure, a humble dignity of bearing."

Sarah Orne Jewett,
THE COUNTRY OF THE POINTED FIRS

A flea-market table, metal chairs, and trees potted in rolling crates add rusticity to an urban view. **OPPOSITE** A 1920's greenhouse has been adapted for morning contemplation, craft projects, and candlelit meals.

"It struck him that the seasons sometimes
gain by being brought into the house,
just as they gain by being brought into
painting, and into poetry."

Willa Cather,
THE PROFESSOR'S HOUSE

No Home Is More Beautiful Than
One in Harmony with Nature

When it comes to living with what you love, consider the external world your field guide for inspiration. Think of the decorative bowls of colored leaves and crimson berries on display in *Sons and Lovers,* the buffalo skins in Willa Cather's *My Antonia,* or the cracked blue jug of apple blossoms in *Anne of Green Gables.* Not all of these accessories will last forever, but that's okay; it's all part of a wabi-sabi approach to style, the time-honored Japanese aesthetic that holds transience in high regard and considers impermanence inseparable from what makes something beautiful.

OPPOSITE This little still life derives much of its power from Henry David Thoreau's entreaty of "Simplicity, simplicity, simplicity!"

CHOOSING AN EARTHY PALETTE

There's nothing more natural than a palette inspired by the great outdoors, but if you don't pay close attention, you can end up with a room that's beige in body and soul. Follow these tips to keep your space from feeling dull or washed out.

- *Establish a calm foundation.* For big pieces like sofas and chairs, choose something in a neutral color like white, brown, or gray so that you can layer with abandon. It's all right if your dining table and your chairs are different shades of brown. Subtle variations in woods add depth to a room and prevent it from feeling one-note.

- *Energize with contrasts.* Tabletop accessories, pillows, and artwork are a great way to introduce color in small doses. If you feel drawn to dense colors, try incorporating pigment-rich accents like persimmon or marigold or apple green to make a brown or gray palette feel even richer. For a more muted option, sage greens, robin's-egg blues, and soft pinks work beautifully with any neutral palette.

- *Amplify with texture.* When your palette is restricted, texture becomes a crucial factor in keeping a room looking interesting. Coarse materials like burlap, wicker baskets, a seagrass rug, or rush matting add a pleasing visual tension to the flat nap of cotton or linen. If your furnishings swing toward the rough side already, then take the opposite route: add something smooth like raw silk or plush like cotton velvet to offset it.

"A work-room should be like an old shoe; no matter how shabby, it's better than a new one."

Willa Cather, THE PROFESSOR'S HOUSE

> "Wreaths of cottage flowers, like chains of little gems, hung from the rafters. Their reds, oranges, blues and pinks glowed against the soft, sooty-black of the ceilings and walls."
>
> Stella Gibbons,
> COLD COMFORT FARM

In *Cold Comfort Farm*, the characters have a kinship with nature that goes far beyond a passing fancy: "[They] live intensely and with a wild poetry," writes author Stella Gibbons. And in *Tess of the d'Urbervilles*, Thomas Hardy writes of people who "preferred sermons in stones to sermons in churches." Like them, you, too, can find artistic inspiration in Mother Earth. A bowl of pinecones mixed with some brilliant fall leaves is all you need to create a seasonal centerpiece. Even the most ordinary of objects deserves a place of honor, so arrange shells and feathers into artful patterns on a table. Remember that a pretty branch leaning up against a wall can have the personality and impact of a painting.

THE MEDICINAL POTTED GARDEN

Back before aspirin and antibiotics, people used natural remedies to treat common ailments like heartburn, colds, and indigestion and landscaped their outdoor spaces to serve such purposes. In *Sons and Lovers*, Mr. Morel has a simple garden full of medicinal herbs like horehound, wormwood, and dandelion. Growing your own herbs for healing teas is a wonderful way to connect to the soil, do something beneficial for yourself, and bring greenery indoors. Below, a list of plants easy to grow in a variety of pots and containers—no backyard required, just perhaps a sunny window.

BASIL
Stimulates appetite, uplifts mood

CALENDULA
Offers antifungal properties good for cuts, scrapes, and insect bites

CHAMOMILE
Calms an upset stomach, settles jangled nerves

HOREHOUND
Reduces mucus in coughs and colds

LAVENDER
Aids with irritability, headaches, anxiety, and exhaustion

LEMON BALM
Relieves sleeplessness and excitability

PEPPERMINT OR SPEARMINT
Relieves stomachaches and sore throats, freshens breath

ROSEMARY
Stimulates circulation, is good for nervous complaints

SAGE
Reduces indigestion, good source of vitamin K

THYME
Improves digestion, helps control coughing, makes an excellent hair tonic

Private viewing: Artwork taped to shelf edges
turns a bookcase into an instant art gallery.

"He made close acquaintance with phenomena which he had before known but darkly—the seasons in their moods, morning and evening, night and noon, winds in their different tempers, trees, waters and mists, shades and silences, and the voices of inanimate things."

Thomas Hardy,
TESS OF THE D'URBERVILLES

A collection of seashells
makes an ever-evolving
family pastime, no
batteries required.

"The stove was very large,
with bright nickel trimmings."

Willa Cather, MY ANTONIA

The Finishing Touches

Have you fallen in love with the plainspoken honesty of this style? Here's a checklist of accessories to bring a rustic feel to your space.

Enamel steel dishware	Braided rugs	Steel apothecary cabinets
Leather cabinet pulls	Wire-mesh food domes	Mason Cash mixing bowls
Wooden pegboards	Nautical landscapes	Vintage wire egg baskets
Pewter jugs	Old daguerreotypes	Leather butterfly chairs
Sailor's-knot doorstops	Gingham	Horn-handled cutlery
Trestle tables	Iron weathervanes	Cork accessories
Seagrass, jute, and apple floor matting	Welsh blankets	Steel Kik-Step stool
Wooden breadboards	Sheepskin rugs	Straw whisks and brooms
Cast-iron cookware	Wool army blankets	Natural-fiber table mats
Duck canvas aprons	Patchwork quilts	Firewood baskets
Glass mason jars	Ammonite fossils	Leather pot holders
	Geode bookends	

Old tin mail pouches are given new life as backyard planters. **OPPOSITE** This glass and wood Chemex coffee maker fits D. H. Lawrence's aesthetic of owning only "solid worthy stuff that suit[s] an honest soul."

"We are all children
of the soil."

Thomas Hardy,
TESS OF THE D'URBERVILLES

Oh, the Glamour of It All

F. Scott Fitzgerald knew what it meant to really inhabit a room. His descriptions of interiors in *The Great Gatsby* and *Tender Is the Night* have a sexy immediacy to them—they capture the feeling that "right here, right now" is all that matters. Fitzgerald isn't the only one who sees the world like this—in novels like Ernest Hemingway's *The Sun Also Rises*, W. Somerset Maugham's *The Razor's Edge*, and Michael Arlen's *The Green Hat*, home is a place where glamour and exuberance collide, clean lines reign, and everything is arranged for maximum reflection. I call it the "glitterati effect": the spirit of confidence born during the 1920s when suddenly people could travel the world for amusement and experience as many of life's fleeting pleasures as possible. In these novels, the art of living well means being tuned in to the glorious potential of every moment. It's chicness, stirred.

"Nicole had designed the decoration and the furniture . . . the pieces reflecting modern tubular tendencies were stauncher than the massive creations of the Edwardians."

F. Scott Fitzgerald,
TENDER IS THE NIGHT

"[She'd] gotten used
to the room with the
soft colors and polished
furniture . . . and all the
intoxication of desire, felt
in so many ways."

Stefan Zweig,
THE POST OFFICE GIRL

Here, Rooms Are Glamorous and Unpretentious in Equal Doses

Like Hemingway, you believe style comes not from showiness but from life's time-honored pleasures: in *The Sun Also Rises*, Count Mippipopolous remarks, "It is because I have lived very much that now I can enjoy everything so well." For you, what counts are the classic comforts of the day's living: a delicious cocktail, a crimson sunset, a gathering of kindred spirits that goes late into the night. A home designed to accommodate moments like this is luxury indeed.

One pigment-rich pop of color is enough to make a room come alive. **OPPOSITE** A memorable space can be as simple as two elements that resonate in an interesting way: here, a bookshelf and a colorful rug play off each other's lines and circles. **PREVIOUS PAGES** Gold wallpaper, an Art Deco sideboard, and a painting by Ione Skye Lee evoke the jet-set world of an F. Scott Fitzgerald novel.

"The cafés were just opening and the waiters were carrying out the comfortable white wicker chairs and arranging them around the marble-topped tables in the shade of the arcade."

Ernest Hemingway,
THE SUN ALSO RISES

Arrangement in black and white: weatherproof polka-dot upholstery lends Gallic flair to an outdoor dining area. **OPPOSITE** A white kitchen with a Carrara marble countertop is always chic and guarantees the food is the main attraction.

The classic bistro chair has a casual chic that feels as at home in a dining room as it does in a Parisian sidewalk café. For the genuine article, check out companies like Poitou, Drucker, and Maison Gatti, which weave their chairs with rattan and Rilsan, a miracle resin that keeps colors from fading. For a slightly more modern option, try the Marais A side chair, designed in 1934 by Tolix. Made of varnished steel, it has a utilitarian charm that's no less sophisticated.

Marble has a unique high-low appeal—it's favored by rulers for building their palaces and by cooks for rolling their dough. In novels like *The Green Hat* and *The Sun Also Rises*, marble tables are the preferred choice for one-size-fits-all lifestyles: they handle everything from fancy dinner parties to slouchy coffee-and-newspapers breakfasts with equal aplomb.

"[There was] cleanliness to the degree
where it becomes an aesthetic element."

Sybille Bedford, JIGSAW

A bar cart is one of those indulgent details that takes gracious living to the next level. In Stefan Zweig's *The Post Office Girl*, as soon as the bellboy enters Christine's hotel room with a "cute little cart on little rubber wheels" stocked with tempting libations, she decides she's never going back to dreary village life. What I love about a bar cart is that you can load it up with drinks and snacks and enjoy the perks of table service no matter where you're sitting. Stock your cart with colored Venetian glasses, which feature heavily in these novels—drinks may or may not taste more delicious in them, but they definitely look better.

"The footman was advancing across the room with a tray containing two green glasses and a little bowl of olives."

Beverley Nichols, CRAZY PAVEMENTS

CORDIALLY YOURS

The next time you entertain, set up a classic cordial bar and let your guests pour themselves an aperitif, or pre-dinner cocktail. Cordial liqueurs taste great on the rocks or with a splash of soda and a wedge of lemon, so it's easy for people to sort themselves out while you carry on with host duties. A few well-chosen liqueurs are all you need to offer up a glamorous sip of the past. Try these:

- *Aperol*—an aperitif with ingredients of bitter orange, rhubarb, and gentian

- *Campari*—a lipstick-colored aperitif made from an infusion of herbs, aromatic plants, and fruit

- *Cassis*—a French black currant liqueur

- *Cinzano*—an Italian aperitif made from fortified white wine

- *Lillet*—an aperitif made with Bordeaux wines and citrus liqueur

- *Luxardo*—an Italian maraschino cherry liqueur

- *Pernod Anise* or *Ricard Pastis*—classic anise-flavored liqueurs

- *St. Germain*—made from fresh elderflowers picked in the French Alps

> "His house when finished was fresh and gay, unusual, and simple with that simplicity that you knew could only have been achieved at great expense."
>
> W. Somerset Maugham, THE RAZOR'S EDGE

Style that looks effortless often comes down to the grandness of simple things. OPPOSITE A room decorated in quiet, soothing colors allows decorative objects to take center stage.

Restraint Is the Key to Elegance

When it comes to a classic wardrobe, the fundamentals apply—good fabrics, clean lines, simple silhouettes, and shapes that flatter—and the same goes for decorating a home. Let well-tailored furniture provide the basic foundations of a room and use stylish accessories to satisfy any design restlessness. From now on, think of well-chosen embellishments like art, pillows, and tabletop accessories as the handbag/shoe equivalents of interior design.

Vintage steamer trunks conjure up porters, valets, and first-class carriages and generate an aura of wanderlust in a room. Before the jet age of travel, luggage was designed for stylishness first and portability second—in *Jigsaw*, Sybille Bedford's glamorous mother is always heading to the South of France

The shape of things: When color is absent, silhouette comes into play. **OPPOSITE** The restricted palette of light and dark steeps this dining room in undeniable glamour. The spiky orb is by Kelly Wearstler.

"[It was] a respectable
old leather case totally
unsuited to air travel, the
kind one inherits from a
father, with half a label
still left from Shepheard's
Hotel or the Valley of
the Kings."

Graham Greene,
MAY WE BORROW
YOUR HUSBAND?

with stacks of "voluminous and unusual luggage." Today, flat-topped vintage
trunks are extremely collectable as coffee or side tables—their craftsmanship
is extraordinary, and their luxurious interior fittings easily adapt to modern-
day uses like storage for CDs, silverware and linens, or out-of-season clothes.
Besides quintessential French companies like Louis Vuitton and Hermès, look
to auction houses or eBay for vintage pieces by Goyard, Moynat, Asprey, John
Pound, Finnigans, and Drew & Sons.

Mirrors are dreamlike conveyors of light and shadow. In *Tender Is the Night*,
Rosemary Hoyt goes to a party in a house lined with "the myriad facets of many
oddly bevelled mirrors" that's a stylish lesson in the power of reflection. Mirrors
transform a room instantly: they can make it feel twice as spacious, bring light
to a dark corner, and sometimes even function as a work of art in themselves.
An antique mirrored backsplash along one wall of a kitchen or home bar makes
a chic serving area during dinner parties and can give a space a Hemingway-
esqe café atmosphere.

ABOVE AND OPPOSITE Vintage
trunks add pre–jet-age glamour
to a room and double as extra
storage.

DINING À LA *TENDER IS THE NIGHT*

The dinner party at Dick and Nicole Diver's hillside villa on the French Riviera is memorable not just for its ultra-glamorous surroundings but for the solicitude with which Dick Diver treats his guests. His old-school manners make a difference: he's right there to greet them, to offer them a cocktail, to make them feel special. Thanks to F. Scott Fitzgerald, we are privy to all the little details that make the evening so enchanting:

"TO BE INCLUDED IN DICK DIVER'S WORLD FOR A WHILE WAS A REMARKABLE EXPERIENCE" The secret to a successful dinner party lies in making other people feel good. It's that simple. How do you do this? By greeting your guests immediately and setting the tone of the evening. By fixing them a drink straightaway. By keeping the meal simple and not experimenting with new recipes, and by switching seats for dessert so everyone gets a genuine opportunity to talk to each other. Dick Diver creates an environment that inspires his guests to be their best selves—what better testament to a host is there?

"HE POURED A COCKTAIL" In *Tender Is the Night*, the characters Dick and Nicole Diver were modeled on expat American jet-setters Gerald and Sara Murphy, who were famous for their signature cocktail called "Juice of a Few Flowers." Their drink was a heady concoction of gin, citrus fruit, sugar, and mint, and recipes for it are easily found online. Coming up with your own house cocktail is a chic way to express your personal style at a party, and knowing you can make it perfectly every time is one less thing to worry about.

"A GRACIOUS TABLE LIGHT, EMANATING FROM A BOWL OF SPICY PINKS" It's hard to beat the theatricality of an underwater flower arrangement. Submerge a pink orchid stem in a cylindrical glass vase and top it with a floating candle. If you don't mind bubbles, use tap water. For a crystal-clear effect, use distilled. To weigh the flower down, tie some clear fishing wire to a small counterweight and then cover it with river rocks.

"A SENSE OF BEING ALONE WITH EACH OTHER IN THE DARK UNIVERSE" Darkness heightens the senses. When you light a dining table, keep the surrounding areas a little shadowy so that the drama is concentrated where you're sitting. It'll give your guests the impression of being at the center of the world, or as Fitzgerald so poetically puts it, "nourished by its only food, warmed by its only lights."

A "PATH EDGED WITH SHADOWY MYRTLE AND FERN" Night gardens, also known as "moon gardens," add a dramatic effect to an outdoor dinner party. White-petaled flowers and silvery fronds like fern and sage look luminous under moonlight, and fragrant night-blooming plants like myrtle, jasmine, and gardenia turn the world into your own scented sanctuary.

"WINE-COLORED LANTERNS IN THE PINE" It's a beautiful image, isn't it—a table and wicker chairs lit from above by flickering red orbs? An assortment of votive-lit lanterns can turn an ordinary back garden into something magical. Look for the ones made of pierced metal that send out a glittering constellation of tiny beams. If you don't have a tree to string lanterns from, be creative: hang them from an awning or dangle them from a wire anchored between opposing walls.

Dark walls and a glittering glass chandelier conjure the drama of a starry sky.

Well, hello there: this entry foyer's sexy attitude comes from its monochromatic palette and the visual tension of all those angles and curves. **OPPOSITE** Gray walls trick the eye into thinking this room is bigger than it is. The white cowhide keeps your attention centrally located.

Where There's Light, There's Dark

Pale colors may reign supreme in glitterati homes, but that doesn't mean anyone is afraid of the dark. The reverse is actually true—where there's light, you'll usually find its tonal opposite. Pairing opposite elements has a way of heightening the unique qualities of each one; it's the juxtaposition that brings these contrasts to life.

"Sylvester's bedroom was all shape and no color. . . . The sun was shining warmly into the room, lighting the limp silver curtains and silvery stripped wood."

Molly Keane, DEVOTED LADIES

Muted colors give this bedroom a sensuous appeal. Grass cloth on the walls adds coziness without sacrificing elegance. **OPPOSITE** For a warmer spin on gold and silver, try flax-colored wallpaper and blue-gray carpet, as seen here in this chic home library.

White rooms sing with light and allow occupants to take center stage. In *Crazy Pavements*, Beverley Nichols writes of an interior "of the palest lemon-colour, with furniture of white leather, lit by the cool silver flame of naked candles." Choosing the right shade of white can be tricky, but in general, whites with a blue undertone work well in contemporary spaces (think art gallery vibe), while shades with a pink or khaki undertone make a room feel warmer and more inviting.

Dramatic color contrasts play an important role in bathing a room with glamour and energy. In *The Good Soldier*, Ford Madox Ford uses black-and-white decor to describe a room's theatricality: "I shall never forget the . . . dining room . . . That white room . . . the tall windows; the many tables; the black screen round the door with three golden cranes flying upward on each panel." It's an effective description of the power of polarity—the result is elegant, a bit edgy, and definitely not for the meek.

OPPOSITE Persimmon walls draw your eye to the objects on this bookshelf.

COLOR: PIGMENT FOR NEUTRALISTS

In *The Good Soldier*, Ford Madox Ford prefers his pigment in small concentrated doses: "The whole world for me is like spots of color in an immense canvas." If you're in the same camp, here are a few ways to take it one step at a time.

- *Add a fabric border to the sides and bottom of your curtains.* It will introduce a stripe of color to a room without feeling overwhelming.

- *Frame some wallpaper.* If papering a whole wall feels like too much, just frame a roll or two. Hanging two or three same-sized pieces at regular intervals can create the feeling of a trompe l'oeil paneled wall.

- *Paint the back walls of a bookshelf.* This will add a focal point to a room, and it's amazing how such a little trick can make your bookshelf look like an art piece in itself. And banish the clutter—it's much better to have shelves that are a little bare than to fill every square inch of them. Otherwise how is anyone going to see that new beautiful color?

- *Add contrasting piping to your furniture.* This is a variation on the curtain border idea and works well with pieces that have a strong shape to them. Welted piping around the edges can make a tired chair or sofa feel fresh again.

"It was dawn now on Long Island and we went about the house opening the rest of the windows downstairs, filling the house with grey-turning, gold-turning light."

F. Scott Fitzgerald, THE GREAT GATSBY

Gold and silver are materials to be reckoned with. In light rooms, they shimmer brilliantly, and in dark interiors, they act as a source of illumination, emitting an ethereal glow. And don't be afraid to mix them (the idea of them clashing doesn't hold up any longer). Metallics are considered neutrals—layering different tones together gives a room the feeling of having been assembled over time instead of purchased in one fell swoop (oh, the horror).

Painting a dark color along the top of a tiled bathroom wall dramatically highlights a collection of classic black-and-white photographs. **OPPOSITE** Lace curtains cast dappled patterns on a dark wood floor. A silvery goat-fur bench provides texture without adding color.

"The Divers' day was spaced like the day of the older civilizations to yield the utmost from the materials at hand, and to give all the transitions their full value."

F. Scott Fitzgerald,
TENDER IS THE NIGHT

The colors of this gold-and-lacquer credenza act as a visual motif for the entire room. **OPPOSITE** Astier de Villatte plates, gold-dipped carafes, and heirloom silver evoke the milieu of *Tender Is the Night*, where every object is given "exquisite consideration."

"Once inside the door there was nothing of the past . . . The outer shell, the masonry, seemed rather to enclose the future."

F. Scott Fitzgerald,
TENDER IS THE NIGHT

The undulations of a gold-colored Eames rocker contrast nicely with a geometric lacquered sideboard. OPPOSITE Pale colors send off prisms of energy and are eternally stylish.

Sleekness Counts

Words like *smooth* and *streamlined* speak to you. Not for you an overstuffed sofa or a patchwork quilt—you're much more at home on a graceful daybed with a taupe cashmere throw. "Modern" isn't a time period, it's an attitude—confident, optimistic, and unflappable. Case in point: the classic Eames rocking chair was designed in 1948, but it has a boldness that still feels fresh today.

In *The Green Hat*, Michael Arlen writes of a slipper chair with a trim modern silhouette. Streamlined furniture like this takes up less visual space, so it's wonderful for opening up a small room and letting the artwork or accessories shine. Plus, gently sculptured shapes are inviting—they soften a room so that it feels more lovable and livable.

Painting your floor, walls, and ceiling in the same color gives the impression of furniture floating in space. **OPPOSITE** Leggy side tables don't steal focus from the rest of a room and provide just enough resting space for one or two special objects.

"She lay on his divan,
silver and bark
geometrically woven into
its fabric."

Molly Keane,
DEVOTED LADIES

Geometric patterns sprung up as a decorative response to Cubism and were all the rage for 1920s trendsetters: in *The Razor's Edge*, Elliot Templeton decorates his house with modern fabrics for a look that "never overstepped the bounds of good taste." Today, having stood the test of time, geometric accents are considered a true design classic. If you're mixing more than one geometric pattern in the same room, stick to ones in the same color range, which will give you depth without looking overly busy.

This bedroom uses a predominantly gray palette to achieve a silvery glow. **OPPOSITE** Dark beams converge on a colorful corkboard that reins artwork and ideas into one space.

"Her naïveté responded whole-heartedly to the expensive simplicity of the Divers . . . unaware that it was all a selection of quality rather than quantity."

F. Scott Fitzgerald,
TENDER IS THE NIGHT

The Finishing Touches

The next time you're on the hunt to add a bit of glitterati cachet to your home, take this list of stylish accessories with you.

Globe match holders

Lacquer boxes

Abstract art

Arco-style lamps

Rolling bar carts

Shagreen, ebony, and alabaster accessories

Colored Venetian glasses

Duralex glasses

Barstools

Laguiole cutlery

Astier de Villatte ceramics and flatware

Wicker-wrapped glass carafes

Zinc metalware

Lace curtains

Midcentury-era vintage globes

Black-and-white polka-dot fabric

Antique glass chandeliers

Côté Bastide tea towels

White leather

Backgammon sets

Lacquered furniture

Gambone vases

Mariages Frères tea canisters

Hanging lanterns

Silver cocktail shakers

Striped canvas beach umbrellas

Pigskin luggage

Black-and-white photography

Zebra-skin rugs

OPPOSITE Every which way but loose: varying rows of books with artwork and antiques helps anchor everything in place and is pleasing to the eye.

"We had loved the big studio with the great paintings. It was like one of the best rooms in the finest museum except there was a big fireplace and it was warm and comfortable."

Ernest Hemingway, **A MOVEABLE FEAST**

Anything Goes

To authors like Isak Dinesen, Virginia Woolf, and Dodie Smith, the real purpose of a home is to foster the flourishing of art, ideas, and people. In their fictional bohemian worlds, characters live with a wild sense of poetry, and their personal spaces reflect it: they're joyful, unorthodox, and fearlessly layered with color, textiles, and stories. Yes, these homes may challenge the rules of convention, but that's exactly why they're so welcoming. Here, personal style isn't about cash; it's about attitude, wit, and making do with what you have. If you know of a place that's always bubbling with conversation, candlelight, and cushions, chances are high that there's a novel by one of the authors in this chapter on its bookshelves.

"The furnishing of his little room suggests a highly eclectic spirit."

Lawrence Durrell,
THE ALEXANDRIA
QUARTET

A swordfish, an Indian daybed, and a vintage chandelier reveal the eccentric passions of the room's owners. **OPPOSITE** Densely patterned rugs, textiles, and a palm tree give this bedroom the atmosphere of a far-off, magical place.

The More, the Merrier

Bohemian rooms encompass all styles and all points of view. They mix things together in ways other people would never dream of: gold vinyl cushions with an antique Indian settee, for instance. This creative all-inclusiveness spills over into guest lists, too: in *My Family and Other Animals*, Gerald Durrell writes of a party filled with so many fascinating people and extraordinary conversations that he doesn't know where to turn first. Rooms designed to stimulate conversation are rooms that people don't want to leave.

"Behind the Verandah, there were collected
many fine Arab and English things:
old ivory and brass, china from Lamu,
velvet armchairs, photographs, and a
large gramophone."

Isak Dinesen, OUT OF AFRICA

Hippy chic: A family's ongoing love affair with travel is reflected in the room's vibrant palette.

"Nothing matched anything else. Everything was of an exotic brilliance that took away the breath. 'Not the room of a lady,' thought Miss Pettigrew."

Winifred Watson,
MISS PETTIGREW LIVES FOR A DAY

Jewel-toned palettes offer a visual high-speed link to far-off destinations. Ruby and turquoise conjure up Uzbek suzanis, brilliant pink takes you nonstop to India, and saffron and carnelian drop you off in front of those enormous spice cones in Middle Eastern souks. Layered together, these tones exude energy and passion: in Lawrence Durrell's *The Alexandria Quartet*, there's a sheik's tent covered in maroon and green stitching, and in Virginia Woolf's *Mrs. Dalloway*, every flower at dusk glows "violet, red, deep orange."

Katherine Mansfield considered a fondness for overlapping patterns a litmus test for whether a person had a creative mind-set or a bourgeois one—in her short stories, characters live in rooms with "terra cotta painted walls with a fringe of peacocks," or have an Indian bedspread with a border "of red leopards marching round it." Besides resulting in a look that's much bigger than the sum of its parts, mixing different textiles together tells people you follow your own design muse and reveals a self-assurance that's blissfully unbounded by public opinion.

Mixing patterns is like being part of a great rock band: each musician may be a genius, but the real magic happens when everyone plays together. If you feel a bit tentative about where to begin, here are a few basic tips for creating relationships that last.

- *Make a commitment.* Fall in love with something and make it your anchor fabric. Choose between three and five colors in this fabric that you would like to see repeated elsewhere in the room.

- *Remember that opposites attract.* Contrast geometric fabrics like ikats, chevrons, and stripes with curvy patterns like florals, toile, and leopard prints.

- *Know that size matters.* A good rule of thumb is to choose one pattern in a large scale, one in a medium scale (half as big as your large one), and one in a small scale.

- *Go wild.* Zebra and leopard prints are the stripes and polka dots of the animal kingdom. Their neutral palette looks great with pretty much everything. Go ahead and use them with abandon.

- *Opt for solids.* If you're hesitant to go full-out bohemian, give your eye places to rest by adding pillows, throws, or other accents in one or two solid colors.

A SIMPLE GUIDE TO LAYERING PATTERNS

"It was to be an Arab salon. Already he was having the coffee table and couches built, and he had bought a beautiful, large cream-colored wool rug for the wall, and two sheepskins for the floor."

Paul Bowles,
THE SHELTERING SKY

A capacious corner sofa spiced up with antique kilim cushions is command central for chilling out. **OPPOSITE** Bohemians are artists at heart; their rooms encompass all styles, all cultures, and all points of view.

Every home can benefit from a central hangout that's multipurpose by nature. Whether your inspiration is a tented pavilion, an artists' studio, or a Moroccan *riad*, the goal is the same: to create a common space where reading, eating, entertaining, and relaxing can all take place together. Friends should feel they're always welcome, just like they do in George Du Maurier's novel *Trilby*:

"[There was] a divan so immense
that three well-fed, well-contented
Englishmen could all lie lazily
smoking their pipes on it at once
without being in each other's way,
and very often did!"

George Du Maurier, TRILBY

"It was furnished as
a sitting room, with
great divans piled with
cushions. . . . On the
walls were enlargements
of photographs . . .
much larger than life"

Dodie Smith,
I CAPTURE
THE CASTLE

"[Other artists] dropped in from neighboring studios—the usual cosmopolitan crew. It was a perpetual come-and-go in this particular studio between four and six in the afternoon."

Lounge seating lends informality to a room—essential for people like the artists in *Trilby* who like to stretch, slouch, and sprawl as much as possible (not for them the confines of a high wingback chair). In *I Capture the Castle*, Dodie Smith describes a photographer's studio in St. Johns Wood with "great divans piled with cushions." Clearly, there's a deep-rooted connection between creativity and being horizontal.

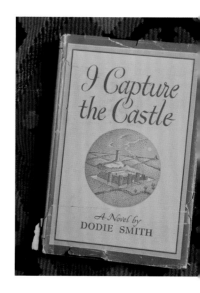

THE ARTY PARTY

Ask any bohemian-minded person why she loves to entertain and she'll tell you it's because it's an opportunity to bring fun and laughter into her home. Below, a few ways to create some wonderful memories.

- *Invite different kinds of people.* As long as your dinner guests share an essential curiosity about life, it doesn't matter whether they know each other or not—curious people ask questions, know how to keep a conversation going, and are usually pretty interesting themselves.

- *Go free-spirited with lighting.* In *The Wilder Shores of Love*, Lesley Blanch writes of Turkish dinner tables clustered with lanterns, tulips, and glass globes of colored water that reflect the candlelight and everything around them. Isak Dinesen loved the picturesque glow of a hurricane lamp: "I remember the things I have seen by [one] better than others."

- *Get creative.* In *My Family and Other Animals*, Gerald Durrell's sister, Margo, makes a tablecloth by drawing enormous murals on "huge sheets of brown paper." You can buy brown kraft paper by the yard at your local art-supply store. Measure the length of your table and buy a piece that's long enough to reach the floor and about a foot more for extra flair. Lay a thick Sharpie next to each dinner plate so guests can unleash their inner artist.

- *Don't tidy up too quickly.* "The table, strewn with napkins and wine-glasses, had a derelict air as they left it." So writes Virginia Woolf in *The Years* about the scene after a particularly fabulous evening. I wholeheartedly agree. When your guests have finished eating, let the dishes linger. Oftentimes, when you clear the table, you sweep the mood away right along with it.

OPPOSITE Fairy lights hanging from a wooden pergola give outdoor dining a starry feel, whatever the weather.

"Great stylists are those
who are least certain of
their effects."

Lawrence Durrell,
THE ALEXANDRIA
QUARTET

Creative Improvising Is the Life Force of Every Room

Enchanting rooms are born when circumstance collides with imagination. As it is for the sisters in Dodie Smith's *I Capture the Castle* who dye their bedsheets green to make them feel new, boredom can be an effective catalyst for mixing things up and reinvigorating a space. Katherine Mansfield believed that a successful room was one that steered wide of conventional design dictums: in her short story "Bliss," she writes of a dining room with daringly unconventional wallpaper, "It was a lovely and gay thing to eat one's dinner at all seasons in the middle of a forest." One last note: it's perfectly all right not to know why you want to decorate something a certain way or not be able to explain a specific design idea. Sometimes it just feels right, and that's enough.

Grouping objects together allows them to form all kinds of new and interesting connections. **OPPOSITE** Replaceable Flor carpet tiles and plywood walls made to be written on make this garage-turned-playroom perfect for creative exploration.

Scattered tubes of paint around a Duncan Hannah work in progress are testament to the importance of disorder. **OPPOSITE** A petite daybed by a window has been re-covered in a busy ethnic pattern for a favorite canine occupant.

Here's the wonderful charm about disorder: a little bit of it makes people feel they can exhale and be themselves. Katherine Mansfield believed unplumped pillows made guests feel more at home. And in *The Years*, Virginia Woolf writes, "He liked Eugénie's drawing room, he thought, as he stood there waiting. It was very untidy." Stack your books on the floor. Tack up postcards in your bathroom. And stop karate-chopping your pillows. Repeat after me: on the other side of perfection lies freedom.

"Picking up the cushions . . . that Mary had disposed so carefully, she threw them back on to the chairs and the couches. That made all the difference; the room came alive at once."

Katherine Mansfield, "BLISS"

"Your life is all wandering,
changes and adventure."

Lesley Blanch,
THE WILDER SHORES OF LOVE

Turn your bathroom into the most interesting room in the house by taping a constantly evolving personal scrapbook of your life to the walls.

Rooms that embrace furniture of all eras and styles feel relaxed and easygoing—they're judgment-free zones. As long as your guiding principle is passion, you'll find a way to make a piece work, and if it ends up fighting a bit with everything else, that's okay; sometimes the less thought-out a room is, the more compelling it becomes. In Gerald Durrell's *My Family and Other Animals*, for example, a pink villa in Greece is decorated with an eccentric assemblage of patterned rugs, colored lanterns, and inherited Victorian furniture—as a character remarks, "Here in Corfu nothing is ever done the correct way." Incidentally, Victorian chaises and daybeds are a perfect fit for sprawling bohemian lifestyles; if you don't feel like re-covering them, just drape them with an ethnic throw.

News flash: a creative DIY attitude is back, so if you don't have something, why not try to make it? In Dodie Smith's *I Capture the Castle*, having no proper furniture for a dinner party is regarded by a character as a test of artistic ability: "Don't worry, we'll manage. It's fun, in a way—a sort of challenge." On-the-spot inventiveness like this is not just admirable, it's exhilarating; as Smith wrote, "I wonder if there isn't a catch about having plenty of money? Does it eventually take the pleasure out of things?"

Redefine your world: a stuffed rhinoceros sculpture created by the owner doubles as a bench for sewing projects. **OPPOSITE** Depth of field: a patterned stencil in the style of the Bloomsbury Group gives dimension to a dining room wall.

Jade walls, citrine curtains, and an amethyst carpet conjure up the bohemian atmosphere of a Katherine Mansfield novel. **OPPOSITE** Over here in the corner: An ordinary built-in cabinet is given a Bloomsbury-style painted makeover.

Rooms Channel Their Inner Nomad

In George Du Maurier's *Trilby*, an artist's studio is decked out with "artistic foreign and Eastern knick-knacks," and Katherine Mansfield characters personalize their spaces with lush ethnic prints and Armenian kilims. Rooms that are a repository of objects the owner has collected over the years offer an intoxicating glimpse into what makes a person tick—you always leave one knowing more than you did when you entered.

No tabletop space? No problem. Here, a hand-painted chair holds a collection of rock crystals. **OPPOSITE** Just like a guest list, art is more interesting when paired with a variety of personalities.

"Everywhere blossomed
the ex votos of the
faithful in strips of
coloured cloth, calico,
beads."

Lawrence Durrell,
THE ALEXANDRIA
QUARTET

What is it about global decor that turns a room into a departure gate for dreams? Is it the desire to travel that exotic objects and souvenirs awaken in us? Or the essential reminder they offer that limits exist only in our mind? In *The Alexandria Quartet*, there's a memorable bedroom decorated with rich Persian rugs, a green Tibetan urn, and "an idol the eyes of which are lit from within by electricity." Rooms like this have a seeker mentality—they inspire us to grow, to wander, and to never stop exploring.

A vintage flag from a San Francisco shipping line makes a colorful headboard for a bedroom with a glass-brick wall. **OPPOSITE** A colorful Indian textile in a bedroom doorway signals that dreams begin here.

Reinvigorate a sofa by layering it with a vibrant *suzani*. Tucking it in gives it an upholstered look. **OPPOSITE** Play and display: electric guitars keep company with JFK paintings casually propped against a wall.

Ideas Are Born to Run Wild

For you, a home needs to be more than a place to relax and be comfortable. It also needs to be part think tank, part workshop, and part laboratory of personal inspiration. Here, rooms don't strive to be perfect, they strive to be interesting—and the place where anything can happen.

Wit can go firmly hand in hand with style, and don't let anyone tell you differently. "Why! Why! Why is the middle-class so stodgy—so utterly without a sense of humor?" bemoans a character in Katherine Mansfield's "Bliss." A few pages on, an interior decorator remarks that she's tempted to redo a client's dining room in "a fried-fish scheme, with the backs of the chairs shaped like

If you've run out of bookshelves, stacking hardcover books vertically makes a bold graphic statement. **OPPOSITE** Burn, baby, burn: Floor cushions and layered rugs make this retro fireplace a groovy hangout.

"In the evenings [Denys] made himself comfortable, spreading cushions like a couch in front of the fire, and with me sitting on the floor, cross-legged like Scheherazade herself."

Isak Dinesen, OUT OF AFRICA

frying-pans and lovely chip potatoes embroidered all over the curtains." This may be an exaggeration, but it's indicative of an attitude that welcomes a bit of cheek and doesn't rein in original thinking.

Exuberant landscaping plays a lovely supporting role in *My Family and Other Animals*. While house-hunting, Gerald Durrell's family visits a villa draped in flowers "as though for a carnival" that proves to be a deciding factor: "As soon

OPPOSITE A window box has been stenciled in a Bloomsbury pattern and planted with favorite wildflowers.

A LESSON FROM THE BOOKS

FLOWERS IN VIRGINIA WOOLF NOVELS

"Real flowers can never be dispensed with," Virginia Woolf writes in *Jacob's Room*. "If they could, human life would be a different affair altogether." She hated stiff formal arrangements and preferred them as natural and unfussy as possible. Below, a few Bloomsbury-worthy arrangements.

- *Float them in bowls.* In her first novel, *The Voyage Out*, Woolf wrote, "What I find so tiresome about the sea is that there are no flowers in it. Imagine fields of violets and hollyhocks mid-ocean! How divine!" By the time she published *Mrs. Dalloway*, she had figured out how to bring this vision indoors: "Sally went out, picked hollyhocks, dahlias—all sorts of flowers that had never been seen together—cut their heads off, and made them swim on the top of water in bowls. The effect was extraordinary."

- *Plant them in moss.* I love wildflowers and highlighted the following passage in *The Voyage Out* when I read it: "The ground was covered with an unmarked springy moss instead of grass, starred with little yellow flowers." How exciting, then, to discover that Woolf fashions this same image into a tablescape in her later novel *The Years*: "There was a bowl of flowers on the table; wild flowers, blue and white, stuck into a cushion of wet green moss."

- *Fan them on walls.* So your walls are a little bare of artwork. Woolf would say, "Not a problem," and offer you this romantic solution from *The Voyage Out*: "There were no pictures on the walls but here and there boughs laden with heavy-petalled flowers spread widely against them."

as we saw it, we wanted to live there." There is something so romantic and hippy-chic about letting vegetation flourish according to its natural wont. Why not let a house's front pillars grow shaggy with vines? Gardens filled with succulent plants or lush trees like banana palms and plumeria are also bewitching possibilities—this wild outdoor poetry lets people know you hold all forms of creativity in high regard.

THE DIY TENTED PAVILION

There's nothing more romantic than an outdoor lounge surrounded by gently swaying curtains à la the "splendid tented-pavilion[s]" of the Bedouin encampments in *The Wilder Shores of Love*, but custom-made draperies are pricey. A friend of mine in Los Angeles came up with an ingenious solution: she draped and nailed five inexpensive painters' drop cloths to her wooden pergola, one on each side and one across the top. She even hot-glue-gunned "pleats" into the fabric—how clever is that? The drapes won't last forever, but at such enormous savings, they don't need to.

"Gates, half-smothered in bougainvillea,
opened rustily into gardens of wild and
unkempt beauty."

Lawrence Durrell,
THE ALEXANDRIA QUARTET

"All the rooms of the house [were] made full of life."

Virginia Woolf,
TO THE LIGHTHOUSE

The Finishing Touches

Now that you know the basic elements of this style, here's a list of specific accessories to create an artful home.

Embroidered door hangings

Flokati rugs

Large floor cushions

Ikat fabric

Vintage Uzbek suzanis

Faded velvet

Leather poufs

Fringed hammocks

Beaded curtains

African juju headdresses

Hand-painted Moroccan ceramic tiles

Moroccan wedding blankets

Beni Ourain rugs

Berber pom-pom blankets

Kilim cushions

Brass samovars

Indian paisley

Hammered copper mugs

Embroidered straw rugs

Mosquito nets for beds

Ammonite fossil plates and bowls

Silk sari curtains

Hanging lanterns

African kente cloth

Cotton fouta towels

Hand-carved window panels

Chinese wedding beds

Papasan chairs

Eastern statues and iconography

African wood stools

Indian hand-painted furniture

Wicker hanging chairs

Brass tray tables

Agate bookends and coasters

Mango-wood tabletop accessories

A tongue-in-cheek sign alerts visitors to leave conservative attitudes at the door. **OPPOSITE** The graceful arch of a magnolia branch left to curve naturally becomes a striking natural sculpture.

"Bohemia, dear Bohemia
and all its joys."

George Du Maurier, TRILBY

Sometimes a Fantasy

For most people, home is a refuge, but for a discerning few it is also a private Xanadu of their own creation. The literary worlds of Marcel Proust, Colette, Oscar Wilde, and others fall under this description, and to enter one of their novels is to be ferried to a strange paradise. Here, nature pales against the brilliance of artifice. The senses overlap—color is something you not only see but also feel. Think of Dorian Gray's opulent Chinese-inspired drawing room or the saturated interiors of Ronald Firbank novels. These rooms not only intrigue, they stun. Maybe it's the walls—some gilded, others upholstered in the finest stamped leather. Or maybe it's the dining table scattered indiscriminately with violets. Whatever it is, you know one thing: you will never be the same again.

"The genius of the room informed her
utterly. She was possessed by it."

Jean Cocteau,
LES ENFANTS TERRIBLES

"So she sat on . . . and
half believed herself in
Wonderland."

Lewis Carroll,
ALICE IN WONDERLAND

Rooms Are Created for Sensory Pleasure

To Marcel Proust, a bed is not just a bed, it's "a cave of warmth dug out of the heart of the room itself." For him and the authors in this chapter, home is a magical Ali Baba's cave of delight that you can't help but be seduced by. In *Les Enfants Terribles*, Jean Cocteau writes of a retreat so bewitching that characters are "unable to resist the spell of [their] upholstered landscape."

An upholstered screen is dotted with antique treasures. **OPPOSITE** Glossy woodwork and walls upholstered in Maharam wool turn this guest room into a Fabergé egg of delights. **PREVIOUS PAGES** A resin and marble hand offers chalk to dinner guests. The glittering crystal insect is actually a light sconce.

"Yellow satin could console one
for all the miseries of life."

Oscar Wilde,
THE PICTURE OF DORIAN GRAY

East meets eccentric in two
magenta Chinese jars and a
bright yellow bergère chair.
OPPOSITE The fierce color
palette in this living room is a
lesson in the art of confidence.

In this highly aesthetic world, color is emotion made visual. Every tone, tint, and tinge must be precisely captured in order to grasp its significance. In *The Child of Pleasure*, Gabriele D'Annunzio isn't content to describe a color as "dull rusty red," he has to specify it's the one "in the pictures of the Early Masters or of Dante Gabriel Rossetti." In *Inclinations*, Ronald Firbank is so painfully sensitive that he uses italics to illustrate the full horror of a holiday catastrophe: "And from there we went to a ghastly hotel where *all the bedclothes were grey.*"

"Properly managed, nothing
need ever clash."

Ronald Firbank, VAINGLORY

"I love beautiful things that one can touch and handle.
Old brocades, green bronzes, lacquer-work, carved
ivories, exquisite surroundings, luxury, pomp—there is
much to be got from all these."

Oscar Wilde, THE PICTURE OF DORIAN GRAY

A modern painting, marble Saarinen table, and colored
Scandinavian glass hold their own against red lacquered walls.
OPPOSITE A red lacquer table attributed to Karl Springer
does double duty as desk and cocktail bar.

Glamour has an irresistible dark side. An orchid is beautiful, but its overripe delicacy and refinement hint at corruption—in *The Child of Pleasure*, a character spies one and exclaims, "What a diabolical flower!" Besides orchids, exotic materials can lend a room the same sensual allure—a tumble of velvet pillows and a fur blanket lazily draped over a sofa practically beg to be touched. Objects with medieval or baroque overtones also evoke a suggestion of sin: in Colette's *Chéri*, there's a brass-bedecked bed "that glimmer[s] in the shadows like a coat of mail."

Black bookshelves give drama to almost anything that fills them. The malachite-and-brass drink trolley adds a bold note of color. **OPPOSITE** This sitting room echoes Odette's apartment in *Swann's Way* with its "dark painted walls" and "lantern suspended by a silken cord from the ceiling."

OPPOSITE Dinner theater:
vermilion lacquered walls impart
a surreal sheen to a marble
Saarinen table and wood chairs.

If You Can Dream It, You Can Do It

Fantasy elements add playfulness to a room and stir one's imagination. In *Self-Portrait with Friends*, Cecil Beaton writes of a painted carousel bed at his country house, Ashcombe, that's "admittedly fantastic and strange with its bright colors and silver trumpery, but to [him], at any rate, infinitely charming."

The real world doesn't hold a candle to the brilliance of the faux. In Joris-Karl Huysmans's *Against Nature*, the narrator prefers shocking colors that look their best under electric light because he lives most of his life after sundown. Big flourishes create big effects, so go ahead and make your own distinctive style statement—a dining room painted in ten coats of red lacquer is one in which conversation will never be dull.

A LITTLE NIGHT DECADENCE

When you bring a group of people together to share a meal, a memorable evening results from more than merely gustatory pleasures. Here are a few ideas to ensure that your atmosphere fosters intimacy.

• *Get theatrical with your flowers.* Nothing's more annoying than having to crane your neck around a barricade of bouquets to see the person sitting across from you. Here are two imaginative alternatives.

  » *Go high:* Take a style tip from Gabriele D'Annunzio's *The Child of Pleasure* and weave a garland of flowers or ivy branches in and out of your chandelier.

  » *Go low:* Steal an idea from Ronald Firbank's *Vainglory* and scatter flower petals on your dining table to strew a little sweet disorder—your guests will think you put more thought into it than you actually did.

• *Keep everyone close together.* Don't worry if your table is a bit small and you have to squeeze in a few extra chairs. Conversation is an ensemble activity, and if people are sitting too far apart, it's difficult to spark any energy or rhythm. Ronald Firbank concurs in *Inclinations:* "Twenty guests, at a table to hold eighteen, insured nevertheless a touch of welcome snugness."

• *Go big before they go home.* Gabriele D'Annunzio believed "the true luxury of the table is shown in the dessert," so if your culinary skills don't extend very far, serve something simple for dinner and save the big finale for the finish. Eton mess (strawberries, meringue, and whipped cream) is incredibly easy to make and always impressive, as is any kind of layered confection served in a glass trifle bowl. Alternatively, order a special cake from a favorite bakery. That way, you'll be sure to end on a sweet note.

"You must *make* your own life as
you would any other work of art."

Gabriele D'Annunzio,
THE CHILD OF PLEASURE

Surreal objects like a stuffed peacock, birds under glass, and an actual oyster bar make this dining room feel curiouser and curiouser. **OPPOSITE** In this decorative wonderland, furniture really does have arms and legs.

There's a haunting splendor to objects that remind us of our own mortality. Taxidermy animals and insects and flowers in a last poetic gasp of life emphasize the transience of earthly pleasures. In *Vainglory*, there's a stuffed and caged canary that's put near a window in order to startle passersby. The poignancy of these objects is what moves us most—we look at a delicate glass jar of mounted butterflies and see a single moment of frozen joy.

"[The aim of life] was to teach man to concentrate himself upon the moments of a life that is itself but a moment."

Oscar Wilde,
THE PICTURE OF
DORIAN GRAY

Just like in *Alice in Wonderland*, a space that pushes the envelope of the status quo is one that leaves an unforgettable impression. Below, a few ways to add a little shock and awe to your rooms.

A LESSON FROM THE BOOKS
THE SURREAL WORLD

- *Put some wings on it.* Insects are a classic Surrealist motif, perhaps because they're so creepy and crawly that they never fail to elicit a reaction. Anywhere you put them is incongruous, so you might as well have some fun. In *Vainglory*, a socialite attaches a huge winged pin to the back of her hair and waits for everyone to flinch. Framed collections of exotic insects, bug-shaped crystal sconces, and brass beetle ashtrays are other ways to incorporate this decorative theme into your home.

- *Add graffiti.* Handwritten scribbles or drawings, as long as they have personal meaning, are a bold and unconventional way to add a graphic element to a room. The siblings in *Les Enfants Terribles* mustachio a plaster head on their mantelpiece, and I have a particular fondness for Cecil Beaton's creative way of memorializing friendship: "Before leaving my house for the first time, [my guests] were made to trace the outlines of their hands on the walls of one of my bathrooms. By degrees, an extraordinary collection was achieved."

- *Make it come alive.* A chair with four legs usually doesn't merit a double take, but a chair with four limbs . . . now, *that's* a conversation piece. Same goes for arms, hoofs, hands, and other extremities. One piece or two is enough to make a statement; otherwise it's apt to become overwhelming, as a character in Ronald Firbank's *Vainglory* bewails: "Such wild herds of chairs; such herds of wild chairs!"

A taxidermy swan chaise by artist Alannah
Currie is the serendipitous embodiment of
a passage from a Proust novel.

"'I am glad you appreciate my sofa,'
replied Mme. Verdurin, 'and I warn
you that if you expect ever to see
another like it you may as well
abandon the idea at once.'"

Marcel Proust, SWANN'S WAY

"'You know you say things are "much of a muchness"—did you ever see such a thing as a drawing of a muchness?'"

Lewis Carroll,
ALICE IN
WONDERLAND

A collection of blue-and-white china is given extra impact with a large gilded mirror behind it. **OPPOSITE** This enchanting breakfast wall is a "living" scrapbook of souvenirs collected from family vacations.

The Only Rule Is More, More, More

Here, there's no such thing as curbing beauty. A green malachite table arrayed with green malachite objects isn't over-the-top—it's making an emphatic style statement. Bedroom walls covered in striped cashmere offer a sensuous surrender to nightly repose. This kind of maximalism celebrates rich colors and ornate details and wrings every ounce of pleasure it can out of every experience.

There's an unbridled luxury to the cashmere dressing gowns and onyx-paved bathrooms in Oscar Wilde's *The Picture of Dorian Gray*, and the fur rugs and rosebud silks in Colette's *Chéri*. Sumptuous textures and materials like these provide immense and immediate joy—why delay gratification if you don't have to? Even small indulgences can amp up the glamour quotient of a room: a lapis lazuli–handled magnifying glass, a velvet pillow, a luxury soap cradled in a small crystal bowl, or a sumptuous faux-fur throw can make all the difference.

On the subject of excess, gold whispers one word: "more." It's sexy and provocative and immediately lets people know you're not fooling around. There's gold woodwork and gilt mirrors and ormolu all over the pages of *The Picture of Dorian Gray*. Gold looks as good against a cool color palette as it does with a warm one and, depending on the type of finish, can emit everything from a soft burnished glow to a high gleam.

Cecil Beaton thought "decorative follies" like these oversized beaded tassels added poetic charm to rooms. **OPPOSITE** Jean Cocteau would have loved the surreal humor of this trompe l'oeil gold table.

A rectangular sofa punctuated by a pair
of circular cushions provides a graphic
backdrop for a gold-leaf table by Yves Klein.

"From pieces of furniture, here and there, came gleams of ivory and mother-of-pearl."

Gabriele D'Annunzio,
THE CHILD OF
PLEASURE

This marquetry table is similar to the one mentioned in *The Picture of Dorian Gray* made "of dark perfumed wood thickly encrusted with nacre." **OPPOSITE** Tiled splendor: mosaics add pattern and color to hardscaped areas and are practically indestructible.

Decorative marquetry, or inlaying furniture with veneers of marble, exotic woods, and other materials, was all the rage among the turn-of-the-twentieth-century elite. In *Against Nature*, a nobleman is so enthralled with the art that he has semiprecious stones set into the shell of his pet tortoise. Look for little tables made with dark wood and mother-of-pearl—their delicate patterns and high contrast add a layer of elegance to any room.

Ah, the mysterious East. It's a signifier for sensuality and worldliness, conjuring up images of souks and harems and opium dens. No wonder then that Dorian Gray's home is filled with "Chinese lacquer boxes with metal-plaited tassels," "blue-dragon bowls," and "silk." And in *Swann's Way*, the reader grasps that Odette is a woman of experience after Proust tells us her bedroom has "Oriental draperies, strings of Turkish beads, and a huge Japanese lantern, suspended by a silken cord from the ceiling." In this world, exotic and erotic are never too far from each other.

banquette and gold octagonal
xy sitting room accommodate
and entertaining by night.

"He had decorated and furnished the public rooms of his house with ostentatious oddity."

Joris-Karl Huysmans, AGAINST NATURE

All the World's a Stage

A good host never forgets that no matter how dazzling the surroundings, the guests are still the stars. A bit of theatricality in your interiors makes people feel attractive and more confident—I like to think it's because they can't help but rise to the sex appeal of the room. Achieving this means examining your space with the eye of a production designer. Where do you want the focus of the room be? Where should the lighting dim? Where do you want people to gather?

Grand Central oyster bar: a cocktail cabinet encrusted with oyster shells gives star power to a dark corner. The peacock is an artful comment on the transience of beauty. **OPPOSITE** A billowing gauze curtain filters light dramatically as a herd of zebra cushions await placement on outdoor sofas.

Appetite for graffiti: dinner parties become a creative confessional with a chalkboard wall. A Currey and Company chandelier casts a dark spell.

"'But [the smoking room] will be rather drastic with all those
strong colors. It's going to look rather charmless without
a lighter note somewhere . . . a white vase or a statue.'
'Nonsense,' [Chéri] interrupted, rather sharply. 'The white
vase you want will be me—me, stark naked.'"

Colette, THE LAST OF CHÉRI

A beautiful object transcends functionality. Rooms that are aesthetically pleasing elevate the senses. In *The Child of Pleasure*, Gabriele D'Annunzio writes of a room so breathtaking that a character stands for a minute "lost in pure aesthetic pleasure and admiration." Dorian Gray's dinner parties are as celebrated for the splendor of his dining table as they are for their guest list, and from Oscar Wilde's description I can see why: they're "subtle symphonic arrangements of exotic flowers, and embroidered cloths, and antique plate of gold and silver."

There's a fathomless mystery to black that makes everything feel a little more dangerous and a little more interesting. Think of the dark painted walls of Odette's apartment in *Swann's Way*. Or the jet-black bathroom in *Chéri*. Or the ebony library bookshelves in *Against Nature*. Black is shadowy and elusive and offers up questions but not so many answers.

"[He had a] passionate cult of the Beautiful . . . [a] keen appetite for the sensuous."

Gabriele D'Annunzio,
THE CHILD OF
PLEASURE

OPPOSITE In a teenager's bedroom, a chalkboard wall takes on a note of goth glamour.

Covering a wall with fabric adds drama and opulence that a coat of paint can never equal. I once draped a wall in gauzy muslin in a studio loft and not only did it make a stunning backdrop, it also created the illusion of a bigger space. I did it the no-frills way and just tacked up my fabric with nails along the top of the wall, but for a more finished look, screw in some antique brass hooks or decorative knobs and have your dry cleaner sew buttonholes at regular intervals along the top edge. Or install a curtain rod along the top of the wall and then drape your fabric from that.

THE DRAPED WALL

CHILDREN'S BEDROOMS: TO SLEEP, PERCHANCE TO DREAM

The colored lantern in the bedroom of the narrator in *Swann's Way* is a wonderful description of how something so simple can spark ideas and fan childhood dreams. Below, a few more ideas which do just that.

- *Put a real knocker on the door.* A brass bird, a lion's head, or an oversized hand lets visitors know they're about to cross into a land that doesn't exist on any map.

- *Go Narnia.* Put a wallpaper mural up on one wall. Choose a forest of snowy trees and lay white sheepskins in front of it. Or cover a wall in chalkboard paint and introduce your child to Harold and his purple crayon.

- *Shake things up.* One mother I know intentionally hangs all the frames in her daughter's bedroom at angles because she wants her to know that there are more ways to look at the world than just straight.

- *Don't forget the ceiling.* Cover it in a colorful swarm of paper butterflies heading south. Or stick on those glow-in-the-dark stars and create a whole galaxy of constellations. Or paint the ceiling blue and hang it with kites.

- *Add some privacy.* If all else fails, a personal tent is the ultimate (and instant) hideaway. Buy one or make your own by attaching a chandelier chain to the ceiling and draping some lightweight shimmery fabric from it. Furnish it with a few pillows and stuffed animals and then tiptoe out quietly. You won't believe how quickly an adventure will spring to life.

The Finishing Touches

For a home that casts a seductive spell and awakens all the senses, keep an eye out for these objects and accessories the next time you go shopping.

Chinese furniture	Porcelain dragon bowls	Murano vases
Gold-leaf ormolu	Crystal balls	Faux ivories
Orchids and chrysanthemums	Fragile gilt chairs	Satin curtains
Decorative insects and butterflies	Acid yellows and greens	Rock crystals
Malachite and lapis lazuli	Japanese Imari vases	Fur cushions
Coral branches	Fabric wall coverings	Cashmere throws
Oversized decorative tassels	Ebony obelisks	Marble busts on pedestals
Lacquer accessories	Turquoise foo dogs	Gilded birdcages
Eggshell china	Metal drinking goblets	Faux tortoiseshell accessories
Bonsai trees	Stamped leather paneling	Vintage candelabras
	Peacock feathers	Coromandel screens

A brass insect encrusted with stones enlivens a spice cabinet. **OPPOSITE** Lushly patterned fabric wallpaper and stacked oil paintings draw your eye to them and not to the Lilliputian-sized room.

A golden mermaid floats above
a copper sink in a kitchen fitted
out with open shelves to hold
dishware and other curiosities.

" Be daring, be different, be impractical, be anything that will assert integrity of purpose and imaginative vision against the play-it-safers, the creatures of the commonplace, the slaves of the ordinary. "

Cecil Beaton,
SELF-PORTRAIT WITH FRIENDS

The Style Gurus

The novels below formed the majority of my research in writing this book. They don't represent the entire output of each author, nor are they in some cases an author's best-known work, but they were for me important touchstones in conceiving the decorating philosophies of each chapter. Think of this reading list as a jumping-off point— whether you're old friends with these literary classics or meeting them for the first time, hopefully you'll be inspired to travel even deeper into these stylish and unforgettable literary worlds.

FROM

"Shall I Put the Kettle On?"

For the following authors, home sweet home is a place where the furniture's a bit faded, the crockery is chipped, and a cheerful domesticity reigns over all.

Louisa May Alcott (1832–1888)

Style inspiration: *Little Women*

The March house in *Little Women* is untidy in a way that enhances its beauty, with books crammed into the recesses, flowers trailing around the windows, and sewing projects scattered on the dining room table. Here, tidying up is done not to impress but to make guests feel more comfortable—plumping pillows, sweeping floors, and sliding the sofa into the warm afternoon light.

Jane Austen (1775–1817)

Style inspiration: *Sense and Sensibility, Persuasion, Emma*

Austen heroines are plucky go-getters who usually have more dreams than cash, and the cottages, parsonages, and manor houses they inhabit embody these same optimistic qualities. When it comes to interior design, pretty trumps perfect, small trumps big, and friendliness trumps formality. As a character in *Sense and Sensibility* puts it, "I advise everybody who is going to build, to build a cottage."

Charles Dickens (1812–1870)

Style inspiration: *David Copperfield, Our Mutual Friend, Bleak House*

In a Dickens novel, a snug home with a crackling fire and a hot supper on the table is the epitome of domestic bliss. Over and over, he reminds us that what matters aren't material possessions but rooms filled with a wealth of cheerfulness and no pretensions to being anything swankier than "an easy dressing-gown or pair of slippers."

George Eliot (1819–1880)

Style inspiration: *Middlemarch, The Mill on the Floss*

George Eliot was a bit of a slacker when it came to domesticity and housekeeping: in *Middlemarch*, she writes cheerfully of a table covered with the remains of a family meal. And when it comes to furnishings, she has a distinct appreciation for jugs with broken handles and carpets with colors that have been subdued by time.

Elizabeth Gaskell (1810–1865)

Style inspiration: *Cranford, North and South, Wives and Daughters*

Elizabeth Gaskell was the household goddess of her day. Her novels are filled with decorating tips for nineteenth-century cottage life, from gathering fallen petals for rose potpourri to the glories of faded chintz to the scented pleasures of an apple studded with cloves.

Kenneth Grahame (1859–1932)

Style inspiration: *The Wind in the Willows*

Open Grahame's cult classic to any page and you tumble headlong into descriptions of cozy kitchens and bright fires and oatmeal porridge and kettles on the boil. The world may be full of peril, but what emboldens the animals on their adventures is the knowledge that whatever happens, home sweet home is waiting—safe, reassuring, and familiar.

Flora Thompson (1876–1947)

Style inspiration: *Lark Rise to Candleford*

In her semiautobiographical novel, Thompson gives a fascinating account of rural life in a nineteenth-century English village. It's a homey place, one where the kitchens have handmade rag rugs, the floors are flagstone, the candles are beeswax, and there's always a pot of geraniums on the windowsill.

Anthony Trollope (1815–1882)

Style inspiration: *Orley Farm, The Small House at Allington*

Though he wrote numerous novels about the rich and famous, Trollope also dug deep into the lives of the humble and unknown to reveal the simple joys of English village life. In *Orley Farm*, for example, he tells us that too much handsome furniture can overpower a room, worn furnishings make one feel more alive, and pretty doesn't necessarily go hand in hand with fashionable. Who can argue with that?

FROM
"Remembrance of Things Past"

These authors believe an elegant home emanates order and harmony, and that traditions and rituals are a gracious way of keeping the past rooted in the present.

Henry Green (1905–1973)

Style inspiration: *Loving*

Loving, Green's novel about domestic servants in a stately country home, is straight out of Downton Abbey land. Its pages teem with fascinating glimpses into a world in which bed linens are aired daily, picnic sandwiches are wrapped in white paper and string, and personal stationery comes with matching colored blotting paper.

Henry James (1843–1916)

Style inspiration: *A London Life*

In James's novel *A London Life*, the characters endure their fair share of trials, but the home they live in is built to withstand disappointment, full of fresh flowers, crisp chintz, quaint maps, and shells in glass cases. Domesticity is the accumulation of little details; they may not seem like much on their own, but all together they can bring contentment.

Thomas Mann (1875–1955)

Style inspiration: *Buddenbrooks*

Buddenbrooks is the story of a German family in transition, and Mann's interiors echo the state of their souls. As the novel progresses, the rooms change from being unyieldingly stiff and formal to being decorated with an eye to art and comfort with worldly influences, low-slung sofas, gentle curves, and light colors.

Nancy Mitford (1904–1973)

Style inspiration: *The Pursuit of Love*

In this semiautobiographical novel, Mitford portrays an upper-class lifestyle as eccentric as it is traditional. At fictional Alconleigh, gold-fringed curtains and rose-covered china live peaceably with heads of beasts on walls, rock collections, and "telegrams announcing casualties in battle." It's all a bit kooky, but that's what makes the home so brilliantly personal.

Vita Sackville-West (1892–1962)

Style inspiration: *The Edwardians*

Vita Sackville-West grew up at Knole House, a "calendar" home in Kent with 365 rooms, fifty-two staircases, twelve entrances, and seven courtyards, and her novel *The Edwardians* is a love letter to her years there. House traditions like personal stationery, bed sheets threaded with satin ribbons, and nightly turndown service testify to the kind of refined hospitality that anticipated every desire.

William Makepeace Thackeray (1811–1863)

Style inspiration: *Vanity Fair*

If you seek dandified decorating tips for your home, look no further than *Vanity Fair*. From trays glittering with glass decanters to sideboards heaving with silver salvers and cruet stands, Thackeray's rooms are as dazzling as his prose.

Evelyn Waugh (1903–1966)

Style inspiration: *Brideshead Revisited*

An intimate of London's Bright Young Things, Waugh had access to a glittering and privileged world. In *Brideshead Revisited*, the Marchmain estate is modeled on real-life Madresfield Court, an aesthetic wonderland of painted parlors, brocade walls, ormolu furniture, and gilt mirrors.

Edith Wharton (1862–1937)

Style inspiration: *The Age of Innocence*

For insight into the characters in a Wharton novel, take a good close look at their homes. Overcrowded brownstones denote stuffy, ponderous Victorian ways of thinking, while houses with pale walls and simple classical accents are code for freshness and modernity. Wharton was so passionate about interior design that she wrote a book about it called *The Decoration of Houses*, still in print today.

FROM
"Living au Naturel"

For these authors, beauty equals simplicity and there is no home so comfortable as the one in harmony with nature.

Emily Brontë (1818–1848)

Style inspiration: *Wuthering Heights*

For Brontë, beauty lay in the unadorned. In *Wuthering Heights*, Heathcliff's manor house is a monument to unpretentiousness with stone floors, hand-carved furniture, and plenty of earthenware. Style inspiration comes from the wild moors surrounding them: the less a home is suffocated in layers of lacquer, the more room the soul has to breathe.

Willa Cather (1873–1947)

Style inspiration: *My Antonia, The Professor's House*

Cather believed in the innate superiority of function over form. To her, possessions were to be valued not for their appearance but for their purpose. In a Cather novel, the floorboards are creaky, the steps are wobbly, and the carpets are worn—but everything performs just fine.

Stella Gibbons (1902–1989)

Style inspiration: *Cold Comfort Farm*

Stella Gibbons wrote with her tongue planted firmly in her cheek. *Cold Comfort Farm* is a comic riff on the testosterone-rich rural worlds of D. H. Lawrence, Thomas Hardy, and others, but beneath all the parody are key characteristics of rustic style. Cameo appearances by twig brushes, old seashells, trestle tables, raftered ceilings, and checked tablecloths should all be duly noted.

Thomas Hardy (1840–1928)

Style inspiration: *The Return of the Native, Tess of the D'Urbervilles*

In the fictional English landscape of Wessex, Thomas Hardy found his spiritual home. *The Return of the Native* offers constant reminders that inspiration starts with the earth. Even a description of brown soil becomes a gentle dig at materialism—if the ground doesn't need more than one layer to clothe itself, Hardy intimates, then why do we?

Sarah Orne Jewett (1849–1909)

Style inspiration: *The Country of the Pointed Firs*

Sarah Orne Jewett was a New England writer who advocated living a simple, self-reliant life. In her best-loved novel, she poignantly records the slowly dying traditions of a small Maine fishing town where residents brew herbs to make medicinal compounds, braid straw mats out of island rushes, and embroider their patchwork quilts with loving stitches.

D. H. Lawrence (1885–1930)

Style inspiration: *Sons and Lovers, Lady Chatterley's Lover, The Captain's Doll*

D. H. Lawrence loathed the dehumanizing effects of big industry and believed man's saving grace was his connection with nature. Resist the allure of the new and shiny, he tells us. There is no home so comfortable as the one in harmony with nature, and fancy silver spoons don't make a meal taste more delicious.

"He was rather proud of his home . . . there was
a simplicity in everything, and plenty of books."

D. H. Lawrence, SONS AND LOVERS

L. M. Montgomery (1874–1942)

Style inspiration: *The Anne of Green Gables series*

There's a profundity in the way the heroine of *Anne of Green Gables* sees her world because her notion of luxury is so achingly uncomplicated. It's as simple as a blue jug full of apple blossom branches and as heartfelt as a table laid with ferns and wild roses. To Montgomery, it's accents like these that transform a house into a home.

Henry David Thoreau (1817–1862)

Style inspiration: *Walden*

Thoreau thought that the more furniture you had in your home, the poorer you were in spirit. In *Walden*, he champions houses built for plain living and high thinking: the less fancy they are, the more room there is for thought to take flight. As long as you have space to think, a house can be small and still feel as extravagant as a palace.

FROM
"Oh, the Glamour of It All"

For these authors, home is a place where glamour and exuberance collide, where clean lines reign, and where everything is arranged for maximum reflection.

Michael Arlen (1895–1956)

Style inspiration: *The Green Hat*

Michael Arlen's cult Jazz Age novel *The Green Hat* is a delicious foray into the importance of laid-back chic. His heroine, Iris Storm, is the archetype for the philosophy that anything worth doing is worth doing stylishly. This means opening your letters with a black ebony paper knife, and drinking vintage brandy out of a gargantuan glass that reaches up to your eyebrows.

Sybille Bedford (1911–2006)

Style inspiration: *Jigsaw*

Jigsaw, Sybille Bedford's novelized memoir about her teenage years in the South of France, is bursting with chic details of streamlined Mediterranean style. Life is simple, sublime, and all about the sophisticated efficiency of whitewashed rooms, tile floors, interesting art, and investing in a few key high-quality items. As she puts it, "[There is] cleanliness to the degree where it becomes an aesthetic element."

F. Scott Fitzgerald (1896–1940)

Style inspiration: *The Great Gatsby, Tender Is the Night*

Fitzgerald's sensibilities are exquisitely attuned to details that charm and elevate. In *The Great Gatsby*, a rose-colored room is bookended by gleaming white French doors and pale curtains, and a party becomes other-worldly when a white garden shimmers with moonlight. Descriptions like this make us attentive to the smallest of moments and expand our appreciation for what glamour can be.

Ford Madox Ford (1873–1939)

Style inspiration: *The Good Soldier*

Hand-stamped pigskin luggage, a crystal globe match holder, a white room with a black paneled screen emblazoned with golden cranes—these are just a few of the modish accents Ford Madox Ford describes for us in *The Good Soldier*, his novel about star-crossed European dilettantes. In this world, every decorative object should elicit a gasp; otherwise, why bother?

Ernest Hemingway (1899–1961)

Style inspiration: *The Sun Also Rises, A Moveable Feast*

In Hemingway's European novels, a handful of tantalizing nouns conjure up an entire atmosphere. Marble-topped café tables and nickel martini shakers evoke the chic world of *The Sun Also Rises*, and zinc bars, wicker chairs, and carafes of cheap white wine depict the artistic milieu of *A Moveable Feast*. Hemingway's design creed is simple: if it's sincere and if it's straightforward, then it's good.

Molly Keane (1904–1996)

Style inspiration: *Devoted Ladies*

Most of the time Molly Keane wrote novels about the foibles of Irish aristocrats; in *Devoted Ladies*, however, she zeroes in on London's Bright Young Things and it's difficult to say which dazzles more, the characters or the

homes they live in. Silver curtains, shiny mirrors, square bathtubs, and geometric fabrics are all gleaming symbols of confidence writ large.

W. Somerset Maugham (1874–1965)

Style inspiration: *The Razor's Edge*

As an expat in the South of France, W. Somerset Maugham was an intimate observer of the jet-set life. In addition, his decorator wife, Syrie, was a champion of the all-white room. Descriptions of pickled furniture, pale silk, and gleaming silver reverberate throughout *The Razor's Edge* and are emblematic of this fresh, forward-thinking sensibility.

Beverley Nichols (1898–1983)

Style inspiration: *Crazy Pavements*

Before fashionistas, there were "modernistas": design-obsessed sophisticates who lived in a perpetual fever for the next great find. In Nichols's novel *Crazy Pavements*, they reside in apartments with pale furniture, black walls, silver ceilings, and bathtubs "apparently quarried from a single block of marble." Here, color is wielded with a careful hand—the wrong tint can be enough to bring on a nervous reaction.

"'You've all been sitting here,' she said, 'for almost an hour, and you haven't noticed my figs, or my flowers, or the way the light comes through, or anything.'"

Virginia Woolf, THE VOYAGE OUT

FROM
"Anything Goes"

These authors believe homes should be filled with art, ideas, and people, and if they're a bit chaotic, well, that's exactly why they're so wildly welcoming.

Lesley Blanch (1904–2007)

Style inspiration: *The Wilder Shores of Love*

Blanch was an inveterate traveler, and her rhapsodic account of four nineteenth-century women globetrotters has an authenticity that comes from personal experience. *The Wilder Shores of Love* is filled with details of far Eastern life *à la bédouine*, a beguiling world with hanging lamps, embroidered tents, and rooftop soirees on cushion-spread terraces.

Isak Dinesen (1885–1962)

Style inspiration: *Out of Africa*

Dinesen fled the trappings of civilization to live according to the dictates of her own heart. In *Out of Africa*, her farm is filled with all the things she loves—history, color, and exoticism. African textiles rub shoulders with English armchairs, Arab antiques, and Danish glass to create a bohemian home that emphasizes friendship and global harmony.

George Du Maurier (1834–1896)

Style inspiration: *Trilby*

Du Maurier's novel *Trilby* is about the artistic free spirits who gave *la vie bohème* its name. Set in fin-de-siecle Paris, their ateliers are designed for the dual pursuit of creativity and pleasure. To that end, sofas are built for three people minimum, walls are decorated with chalk caricatures, and exotic knickknacks, rugs, and textiles are strewn everywhere.

Gerald Durrell (1925–1995)

Style inspiration: *My Family and Other Animals*

Durrell's trilogy (the other two books are *Birds, Beasts and Relatives*, and *Fauna and Family*) is a rhapsodic testament to the charms of disorder. When an English family decamps to a flowery pink villa on a remote Greek island, the furniture is ragtag, colored lanterns hang everywhere, and for dinner parties, murals on brown paper double as tablecloths. With a combination of carelessness and nonchalance, they pull it off: as one character puts it in *My Family and Other Animals*, "Here in Corfu . . . *anything* can happen."

Lawrence Durrell (1912–1990)

Style inspiration: *Justine, Balthazar, Mountolive, Clea*

In his four-novel masterpiece *The Alexandria Quartet*, Durrell writes of a world that engages all the senses. Antique Bokhara rugs share space with Buddha statues, beaded curtains sway seductively in the hot wind, and the scent of lemon lingers over everything. It's erotic and slightly dangerous and wholly appealing.

Katherine Mansfield (1888–1923)

Style inspiration: *"Bliss," "Feuille d'Album," "Psychology," "Marriage à la Mode"*

Katherine Mansfield abhorred the generic taste of the middle class and believed that when it came to design, you had to follow your instincts. Her stories about European bohemians are steeped in decorative details like orange lampshades, Armenian kilim cushions, and Indian print curtains; and if you need confirmation that karate-chopped pillows look stodgy, read her short story "Bliss."

Dodie Smith (1896–1990)

Style inspiration: *I Capture the Castle*

In her cult novel about a penniless English family living in a tumbledown castle, Dodie Smith conjured one of the most enchanting homes ever written about. When it comes to decorating, improvising is their modus operandi. Junk shop furniture is painted to imitate marble, curtains become tablecloths, and a henhouse door is turned into a bench. It's quirky, off-the-wall, and utterly endearing.

Virginia Woolf (1882–1941)

Design inspiration: *The Voyage Out, Mrs. Dalloway, The Years, To the Lighthouse*

Woolf believed passionately in the importance of an uncontrived life. In her novels she reminds us that beauty comes from the smallest of moments—a bunch of sweet peas in a bowl of water, billowing yellow curtains, candles, dogs, canaries. Life happens in the exhale, and the more we are able to relax, the richer and more absorbing our experiences will be.

FROM
"Sometimes a Fantasy"

For these authors, home is a place of drama, dreams, and living to the very edge of one's fantasies.

Cecil Beaton (1904–1980)

Style inspiration: *Self-Portrait with Friends*

Beaton was a renaissance man—photographer, writer, aesthete—and this memoir on living a stylish life is as enchanting as any novel (which is why I've included him). In decorating Ashcombe, his country house, he used money-saving tricks learned from his days as a set designer to create a magical retreat filled with decorative follies like circus murals and faux antiques, and embodying everything he valued: creativity, friendship, and ingenuity.

Jean Cocteau (1889–1963)

Style inspiration: *Les Enfants Terribles*

In *Les Enfants Terribles*, a brother and sister transform their Parisian apartment into a theatrical set piece that becomes their entire universe. Although the story ends in a Greek tragedy, the surreal dreamscape the siblings created for themselves lingers. As Cocteau puts it, "it was indubitably a masterpiece these children were creating . . . the masterpiece of their own being."

Colette (1873–1954)

Style inspiration: *Chéri, The Last of Chéri*

When it comes to pleasure, Colette was a woman who lived to tell. Her two *Chéri* novels offer an exclusive glimpse into the private world of a mature courtesan and her boy-toy lover, and she writes with an attention to sensuous detail—Morocco leather, watered silk, walls painted midnight blue to show off a stark naked occupant—that brings sexy back.

Gabriele D'Annunzio (1863–1938)

Style inspiration: *The Child of Pleasure*

D'Annunzio was a voluptuary who loved to be surrounded by beautiful things and beautiful women. In *The Child of Pleasure*, the rooms he describes vibrate with visual tension: a stone dressing table holds fragile glass bottles, for example, and an iron candelabra is bedecked with a delicate garland of camellias—male versus female energy at its most elemental.

Ronald Firbank (1886–1926)

Style inspiration: *Vainglory, Inclinations*

Firbank's mannered stories of European social climbers may be light on plot, but they're heavy on design tips, like the effectiveness of a dark background for displaying artwork, wiring flowers so they don't wilt, and painting a greenhouse an exotic shade of eau de nil. And you can't beat his all-inclusive color philosophy: "Properly managed, nothing need ever clash."

Joris-Karl Huysmans (1848–1907)

Style inspiration: *Against Nature*

For pure decadence, nothing equals *Against Nature*. The tale of an aristocrat on an all-consuming quest for beauty, the novel has been gathering a passionate audience ever since it was published—even Dorian Gray is obsessed with it. The interiors are excessive beyond imagining, full of exotic furnishings, strange colors, and hermetically sealed scented rooms. Any design lover will be hooked.

Marcel Proust (1871–1922)

Style inspiration: The entire *Remembrance of Things Past* series

Stamped velvet armchairs, dark painted walls, and hothouse flowers are what people mean when they talk about a Proustian world. The atmosphere conjured up in *Swann's Way* is lush and evocative, and images contain an infinite number of associations—one object unlocks a memory of something else, which reminds you of something else, ad infinitum.

Oscar Wilde (1854–1900)

Style inspiration: *The Picture of Dorian Gray*

To Wilde, a beautifully decorated home elevated the mind and was an indication of the artistic temperament that resided within. In his only novel, *The Picture of Dorian Gray*, he gives us glorious visions of yellow satin, Japanese screens, lacquered walls, and dragon bowls filled with exotic flowers. Never satisfied with the ordinary, Wilde believed that an aesthetically rich life was the greatest of the arts.

WITH GRATITUDE

To my incredible blog readers, whose curiosity, conversation, and support have made writing *Novel Interiors* a huge source of pleasure. You are a tribe of kindred souls, and this book would not exist without you.

To Deborah Ginocchio, whose invitation to speak at the Cincinnati Mercantile Library sparked the idea for this book.

To Nicola Beauman, who introduced me to her daughter Francesca Beauman-Bobin, who sent my book proposal to Clare Conville, who gave it to wunderkind literary agent Carrie Kania, who passionately championed it to editor Angelin Borsics at Random House/Clarkson Potter, who taught me how writing a book works, assembled a wonderful production team (hello, Ashley Tucker), and enthusiastically shepherded the manuscript through its long gestation. And to editors Camaren Subhiyah and Amanda Englander, whose stylish stewardship has made all the difference.

To Ivan Terestchenko, the French surfer reincarnation of Cecil Beaton, whose beautiful photographs bring this book to life in the most stirring way.

To the owners of the homes that so beautifully illustrate the modern style and spirit of their literary chapters: Maurizio and Kathleen Almanza, Isabelle Dahlin and Brandon Boudet, Sasha Emerson, the dearly missed John Gibbons, Carrington and Carlos Goodman, Duncan Hannah and Megan Wilson, Christopher Knight and Carlos Aponte, Chelsea and Alex Matthews, Kimberly and Michael Muller, Max Mutchnick and Erik Hyman, Dean Parisot, Meeno and Ilse Peluce, Christos Prevezanos, Shiva Rose, Olga and Eric Roth, Schuyler Samperton, Mark D. Sikes, Michael Silber, Constance and Eric C. Silverman, Marjorie Skouras and Bruno Bardavid, Claire Stansfield and Speaks, Susan Stella, Camilla and Benjamin Trigano, Jeanne Tripplehorn and Leland Orser, and Gary Ventimiglia and David Weinberg. You rock!

To my fellow bloggers who have created such inspiring virtual salons of their own: A Super Dilettante, Vicky Archer, Courtney Barnes, Bart Boehlert, Dominique Browning, Ronda Rice Carman, Heather Clawson, Reggie Darling, Katie Denham, Christian May, Maryam Montague, Slim Paley, Eddie Ross, Patricia Shackelford, Patricia Gaye Tapp, the elusive Tavarua, Sunday Taylor, Pamela Terry, Simon Thomas, Patricia Van Essche, and Scot Meacham Wood.

To David Netto, Diane Dorrans Saeks, Alek Keshishian, and Alex Spak, whose brilliance, erudition, and wit keep me trying harder.

To Alexandra Abramian, Ingrid Abramovitch, Jenny Comita, Yolanda Edwards, Kate Forte, Christopher Hyland, Kyle Marshall, Susan Michals, and Miguel-Flores Vianna, whose early support of my blog *A Bloomsbury Life* made all the difference.

To Martha Adams, Jane Brannigan, Hope Biller, Maya Brenner, Amanda Demme, Janet Eisenberg, Amanda Eliasch, Teri Goldberg, Carrington Goodman, Jenni Konner, Claudia Kremen, Karin Labby, Lucy Lean, Sue Naegle, Liz Naftali, Liz Netto, Stephanie Pesakoff, Olga Roth, Gabrielle Samuels, Suze Yalof Schwartz, Clare Sebenius, Leslie Stevens, Barbara Tehranchi, and Bumble Ward, whose friendship means the world to me.

To Professor Bert Hornback, whose semester-long study of Charles Dickens at the University of Michigan did nothing less than alter the trajectory of my life.

To Belinda Carlisle, my modern-day Lesley Blanch, whose curiosity, passion, and bravery have inspired me for the last fifteen years.

To Hillary Seitz, whose fierce enthusiasm and unflagging friendship during this project was my mast in the storm.

To Jeanne Tripplehorn, whose joie de vivre keeps me sane, and whose thirst for knowledge ensures I always have one foot in the twenty-first century.

To Piero and Luca, who make me tick.

To my siblings, Erik, Brenda, Georgia, Jeffrey, and Philip, and their bright shiny families, who always lift me up.

And last and most important, to my parents, Donna Lou Barion and Arne Magnus Borgnes, who championed my dreams, drove me to and from the public library, and always let me read late into the night.

Beauty's Where You Find It

As I was researching this book, I kept a detailed running list of all the furniture, textiles, and other accessories I felt would be important in helping you to incorporate the gracious details from your favorite novels into your own home. Needless to say, that list got pretty long! Below, the websites, shops, and suppliers whose wares fit the design style and decorating philosophies of each chapter.

Shall I Put the Kettle On?

ANCIENT INDUSTRIES
Brown Betty teapots, straw whisks, spurtles
ancientindustries.com/shop

ANTHROPOLOGIE
Vintage-inspired kitchenware, tabletop items, accessories
www.anthropologie.com

BEN PENTREATH
Home accessories, furniture, prints, antiques
www.benpentreath.com

DASH AND ALBERT
Colorful all-purpose rugs
www.dashandalbert.com

EMMA BRIDGEWATER
Cottage-inspired ceramic ware
www.emmabridgewater.co.uk

FORTNUM & MASON
Kitchen textiles, bakeware, and more
www.fortnumandmason.com

LIBECO HOME STORES
Belgian table and bed linens
www.libecohomestores.com

POTTERY BARN
Sisal rugs, baskets and trays, decorative accessories
www.potterybarn.com

SUMMERILL & BISHOP
Vintage bread tins, traditional kitchenware
www.summerillandbishop.com

Remembrance of Things Past

ABC CARPET AND HOME
Global rugs and antiques
https://www.abchome.com

CIRCA LIGHTING
Lighting collections from top interior designers
www.circalighting.com

HARBINGER LA
Sister Parish wallpaper, Bunny Williams furniture
www.harbingerla.com/home

HOLLYHOCK
Antiques, furniture, fabrics, home accessories
hollyhockinc.com

JAYSON HOME
Modern and vintage furnishings with a global edge
www.jaysonhome.com

JOHN DERIAN
Decoupage trays, tabletop accessories
www.johnderian.com

LEE INDUSTRIES FURNITURE
(available through Crate & Barrel)
Low tufted sofas and chairs
www.crateandbarrel.com

RESTORATION HARDWARE
Salvaged oak tables
www.restorationhardware.com

SERENA & LILY
Bedding, linen, storage baskets
www.serenaandlily.com

WILLIAM YEOWARD
Glassware, decanters
www.williamyeowardcrystal.com

Living au Naturel

COMMUNE DESIGN
Handcrafted goods, table linens, housewares
www.communedesign.com/shop

HEATH CERAMICS
Pottery dining ware, heavy linen tablecloths
www.heathceramics.com

KAUFMAN MERCANTILE
Well-designed cookware, baskets, vintage-inspired accessories, and more
kaufmann-mercantile.com

MOTHOLOGY
Vintage-inspired tabletop items, lighting, art, and accessories
www.mothology.com

OLD FAITHFUL SHOP
Quality kitchen, bath, and pantry goods for everyday living
oldfaithfulshop.com

REJUVENATION
Rustic furniture and accessories
www.rejuvenation.com

RESTORATION HARDWARE
Salvaged furniture, linen, and burlap chairs
www.restorationhardware.com

SCHOOLHOUSE ELECTRIC AND SUPPLY
Classic period light fixtures and home accessories
www.schoolhouseelectric.com

TERRAIN
Garden decor, outdoor living items, kitchen and dining goods
www.shopterrain.com

WEST ELM
Good rustic kitchenware and breadboards
www.westelm.com

Oh, the Glamour of It All

CIRCA LIGHTING
Polished metal lamps, sconces, chandeliers
www.circalighting.com

DWELL STUDIO
Graphic bedding, curvy streamlined furniture
www.dwellstudio.com

ECCOLA
Eclectic, modern Italian vintage furniture
www.eccolaimports.com

GRACE HOME FURNISHINGS
Sleek chairs, tables, bedroom furniture
www.gracehomefurnishings.com

HOLLYWOOD AT HOME
Textiles, home furnishings, vintage pieces
www.hollywoodathome.com

JONATHAN ADLER
Brass, silver accessories, and lighting
www.jonathanadler.com

KNOLL
Midcentury classic furniture
www.knoll.com

MAHARAM
Geometric upholstery fabrics
www.maharam.com

MAISON MIDI
European café furniture, accessories
www.maison-midi.com

STAMPA
Limited edition archival art prints
www.stampa.us.com

Anything Goes

ANTHROPOLOGIE
Colorful patterned furniture and bedding
www.anthropologie.com

HOLLYWOOD AT HOME
Ethnic-inspired textiles
www.hollywoodathome.com

JOHN DERIAN
Moroccan poufs, brass trays
www.johnderian.com

JOHN ROBSHAW
Indian block-print bedding
www.johnrobshaw.com

JUST SCANDINAVIAN
Josef Frank textiles
www.justscandinavian.com

LIBERTY OF LONDON
Rugs, colorful fabrics, antique imported furniture
www.liberty.co.uk

MOTHOLOGY
Kantha throws, pillows
www.mothology.com

NATHAN TURNER
Kilims, vintage and globally sourced furniture
nathanturner.com

SECONDHAND ROSE
One-of-a-kind vintage wallpaper
www.secondhandrose.com

WEST ELM
Ikat cushions, rugs, globally sourced furniture
www.westelm.com

Sometimes a Fantasy

BLACKMAN CRUZ
Offbeat curiosities for discerning collectors
blackmancruz.com

CHRISTOPHER HYLAND
Luxury fabrics for the home
www.christopherhyland.com

CREEL AND GOW
Taxidermy, coral, minerals, and other chic oddities
www.creelandgow.com

1ST DIBS
Global luxuries and antiques
www.1stdibs.com

GRAHAM AND GREEN
Mother-of-pearl furniture
www.grahamandgreen.co.uk

HOUSE OF HACKNEY
Dramatic wallpaper, fabrics, and more
www.houseofhackney.com

JF CHEN
One-of-a-kind European vintage pieces
www.jfchen.com

LIBERTY OF LONDON
Bespoke furniture pieces
www.liberty.co.uk

MARJORIE SKOURAS DESIGN
Chandeliers, mirrors, and seating
www.marjorieskourasdesign.com

PLANTATION DESIGN
Vintage and modern home goods
www.plantationdesign.com

Location Credits

SHALL I PUT THE KETTLE ON?
Isabelle Dahlin and Brandon Boudet
    Los Angeles, California
Sasha Emerson
    Los Angeles, California
Dean Parisot
    Los Angeles, California
Olga and Eric Roth
    Los Angeles, California
Constance and Eric Silverman
    Bernardsville, New Jersey

REMEMBRANCE OF THINGS PAST
Carrington and Carlos Goodman
    Los Angeles, California
Max Mutchnick and Erik Hyman
    Los Angeles, California
Christopher Knight and
    Carlos Aponte
    Jersey City, New Jersey
Mark D. Sikes
    Los Angeles, California

LIVING AU NATUREL
Shiva Rose
    Los Angeles, California
Claire Stansfield and Speaks
    Los Angeles, California
Susan Stella
    Santa Barbara, California
Gary Ventimiglia and David Weinberg
    Los Angeles, California

OH, THE GLAMOUR OF IT ALL
Maurizio and Kathleen Almanza
    Los Angeles, California
Chelsea and Alex Matthews
    Los Angeles, California
Christos Prevezanos
    Los Angeles, California
Jeanne Tripplehorn and Leland Orser
    Los Angeles, California

ANYTHING GOES
Duncan Hannah and Megan Wilson
    New York, New York
Kimberly and Michael Muller
    Los Angeles, California
Meeno and Ilse Peluce
    Los Angeles, California
Schuyler Samperton
    Los Angeles, California
Camilla and Benjamin Trigano
    Los Angeles, California

SOMETIMES A FANTASY
John Gibbons
    Los Angeles, California
Michael Silber
    New York, New York
Marjorie Skouras and Bruno Bardavid
    Los Angeles, California

Index